SEW EASY
papercrafting

REBEKAH MEIER

NORTH LIGHT BOOKS
CINCINNATI, OHIO

WWW.ARTISTSNETWORK.COM

DEDICATION

To my wonderful husband, Brad—without your love and support, I would not get through those sometimes hectic days! Also to my boys, Dan and Matt—your humor and love keep me going.

Sew Easy Papercrafting. Copyright © 2006 by Rebekah Meier. Manufactured in China. All rights reserved. The patterns and drawings in the book are for personal use of reader. By permission of the author and publisher, they may be either hand-traced or photocopied to make single copies, but under no circumstances may they be resold or republished. It is permissible for the purchaser to make the projects contained herein and sell them at fairs, bazaars and craft shows. No other part of this book may be reproduced in any form or by any electronic or mechanical means including information storage and retrieval systems without permission in writing from the publisher, except by a reviewer, who may quote a brief passage in review. Published by North Light Books, an imprint of F+W Publications, Inc., 4700 East Galbraith Road, Cincinnati, Ohio 45236. (800) 289-0963. First edition.

10 09 08 07 06   5 4 3 2 1

Distributed in Canada by Fraser Direct
100 Armstrong Avenue
Georgetown, ON, Canada L7G 5S4
Tel: (905) 877-4411

Distributed in the U.K. and Europe by David & Charles
Brunel House, Newton Abbot, Devon, TQ12 4PU, England
Tel: (+44) 1626 323200, Fax: (+44) 1626 323319
E-mail: mail@davidandcharles.co.uk

Distributed in Australia by Capricorn Link
P.O. Box 704, S. Windsor, NSW 2756 Australia
Tel: (02) 4577-3555

EDITOR: Jennifer Fellinger
DESIGNER: Marissa Bowers
LAYOUT ARTIST: Kathy Gardner
PRODUCTION COORDINATOR: Greg Nock
PHOTOGRAPHERS: Christine Polomsky, Tim Grondin and Al Parrish
PHOTO STYLIST: Jan Nickum

Library of Congress Cataloging-in-Publication Data
Meier, Rebekah
  Sew easy papercrafting / Rebekah Meier.-- 1st ed.
    p. cm.
  Includes index.
  ISBN-13: 978-1-58180-772-1 (pbk. : alk. paper)
  ISBN-10: 1-58180-772-4
  1. Paper work. I. Title.
  TT870.M398 2006
  745.54--dc22
                      2005036596

fw
F+W PUBLICATIONS, INC.

METRIC CONVERSION CHART

TO CONVERT	TO	MULTIPLY BY
Inches	Centimeters	2.54
Centimeters	Inches	0.4
Feet	Centimeters	30.5
Centimeters	Feet	0.03
Yards	Meters	0.9
Meters	Yards	1.1
Sq. Inches	Sq. Centimeters	6.45
Sq. Centimeters	Sq. Inches	0.16
Sq. Feet	Sq. Meters	0.09
Sq. Meters	Sq. Feet	10.8
Sq. Yards	Sq. Meters	0.8
Sq. Meters	Sq. Yards	1.2
Pounds	Kilograms	0.45
Kilograms	Pounds	2.2
Ounces	Grams	28.3
Grams	Ounces	0.035

ABOUT THE AUTHOR

REBEKAH MEIER lives with her husband, Brad, and two sons, Dan and Matt, in northern Illinois, where she fulfills her lifelong passion for creating. A member of the Society of Craft Designers, Rebekah regularly teaches crafting classes. She has been published in several craft magazines and is a regular contributor to *Create & Decorate* magazine. Rebekah is also the author of *Romantic Weddings*, another North Light book.

ACKNOWLEDGMENTS

To the team at North Light—this book would not be if not for the hard work of every one of you, and I thank you from the bottom of my heart. You have made my dreams come true! Thank you, Tricia Waddell, Christine Doyle and Tonia Davenport, for asking me to write my second book with North Light. Special thanks to my friends, editor Jenny Fellinger and photographer Christine Polomsky—you guys are the best! Your talents never cease to amaze me.

TABLE OF CONTENTS

P. 16

CARDS AND STATIONERY

P. 46

BOXES, TINS AND POUCHES

BOOKS AND JOURNALS

FRAMES AND WALLHANGINGS

START STITCHING!

" Whether you've just discovered the joy of crafting or you've been at it for years, you probably have your own favorite crafting mediums—those materials that you can't resist using because they never cease to inspire you. For me, those favorites are fabric and paper. In *Sew Easy Papercrafting*, I've had the opportunity to combine these two mediums. "

LIKE MANY OF YOU, I FIND crafting to be a never-ending source of enjoyment. It is always a pleasure to meet fellow crafters who share my passion and enthusiasm for creative pursuits, and it is fun to learn which tools and materials they most treasure. Whether you've just discovered the joy of crafting or you've been at it for years, you probably have your own favorite crafting items—those materials that you can't resist using because they always inspire you. For me, those favorites are fabric and paper. In *Sew Easy Papercrafting*, I've had the opportunity to combine these two mediums.

I love to coordinate everything, so I was drawn to the idea of being able to use both fabric and paper, mixing and matching as desired to create one-of-a-kind projects! Of course, I used other materials in addition to fabric and paper. But I chose materials that are accessible, simple to use and easy to find at craft, fabric and scrapbook stores. Some of these materials are products that traditionally have been used for fabric, such as fusible web and sewing notions, which I then combined with paper. Others are everyday items that have been transformed into useful or artful objects. (Who would guess a cigar box lid could become a beautiful frame? Or that old blue jean pockets could serve as book covers?) I hope that this eclectic selection of materials inspires you to swing the doors of creativity wide open.

As you might have guessed from the title, most of these projects have some kind of sewing component. You might be thinking, "But I'm a crafter, not a seamstress." Don't worry! I have designed the projects to be enjoyed by crafters of all skill levels. So, whether you are sewing by machine or by hand, whether you are a beginner or an old pro, whether you are a quilter or a paper artist, you will find these projects very easy and fun to create. And, after discovering the world of fabric, ribbons and sewing notions, you will be "itchin' to start stitchin'"!

Have fun creating!

REBEKAH

Materials and Tools

The projects in this book call for a wide selection of tools and materials, many of which are common crafting supplies. Here, I've listed the tried-and-true items that I use the most.

PAPER

There is an ever-growing selection of beautiful paper available at local craft, scrapbook, specialty paper, and office supply stores. The coordinating sets and color schemes now available make it easy to mix and match. These are some of my favorite kinds of paper:

Fabric papers are sheets of fabric that have been specially treated for a stiff, crisp finish. This prevents fraying so that the fabric can be used like paper.

Cardstock is used for several projects in this book. I like to make greeting cards from standard-weight cardstock.

Rice paper, which is made from rice grass, is very thin and tissue-like in appearance.

Tissue paper can be found at craft stores, but I like to save and recycle the tissue that comes in gift boxes.

Manila folders are very versatile. They work especially well for envelopes and patterns.

Chipboard is sold in packages and can be purchased in the art section of the craft store. Gift boxes and empty cereal boxes can be used in place of chipboard.

Foamcore board is a great staple to have on hand. Available in different thicknesses, foamcore is best cut with a craft or hot knife.

FABRIC

The fabrics I use throughout this book can be found at quilting, fabric or craft stores. Typically, fabric is purchased by the yard. Many craft stores sell "fat quarters" of fabric, too. A fat quarter is a piece of fabric that is made by cutting ½ yard in half vertically, making the overall size 18" x 22" (46cm x 56cm). Fabrics come in a wonderful variety of styles, textures, patterns and weights. Here are just a few of your options:

Muslin is a plain, usually undyed cotton fabric. Some muslin comes already "tea-dyed" for a vintage look.

Cotton prints come in various styles and colors, and are frequently sold in fat quarters.

Barkcloth is a vintage-style fabric that was popular in the 1930s, 1940s and 1950s. This medium-weight fabric has a rough surface that resembles the bark of a tree.

Batting is the middle "sandwich" material used in quilting. There are many types and weights available, but I use needled cotton batting for most projects.

Felt is a nonwoven cloth made by matting, condensing and pressing fibers together. Felt is available in wool and also synthetic fibers.

EMBELLISHMENTS

Embellishments not only dress up a project, but they can also give it a one-of-a-kind look. Because the projects in this book have a sewing theme, most of the embellishments I use are sewing-related and can be found in fabric stores. For vintage embellishments, such as old lace and buttons, try garage sales, estate sales, flea markets and online sales. Below are the embellishments I favor—you can add your own favorites to the list!

Lace, ribbon and **ric-rac** are available for purchase by the yard or by the reel. They can be either sewn or glued to projects. There are many types of ribbon available, but I use mostly satin, grosgrain, jacquard and organdy for the projects in this book.

Thread is a must-have for both machine and hand stitching. Button/craft thread is strong and used for hand sewing; Coats & Clark is always a reliable brand. For machine-stitched projects, I use Gutermann 100 percent 100mm polyester thread.

Embroidery floss, available in many colors, is sold in six-strand bundles. Most projects in this book call for three strands of floss.

Beads and **buttons** add an instant accent to any project. And, with so many styles and colors available, you can find beads and buttons to match the look of almost any project. When sewing buttons to a project, use button/craft thread for added security.

Stickers, eyelets, brads, paper clips and **other miscellaneous items** are great embellishments, easily found in scrapbook and office supply stores. Try experimenting and using them in nontraditional ways.

Manila tags make great bookmarks and gift tags. For a special touch, they can be tea-dyed with ink or dye.

Letters and **monograms,** such as stencils, stamps and iron-on transferable letters, are very easy to apply and offer great results. They can be purchased at fabric or craft stores.

RUBBER STAMPS AND INKS

Rubber stamps offer an easy means of beautifying your projects. Both stamps and ink pads, briefly described here, are readily available from craft and scrapbook stores and online suppliers.

Rubber stamps come in a wide assortment of designs, with nearly every image or text imaginable. To ensure longevity of the stamp, be sure to clean the rubber surface with unscented baby wipes after using.

Inks are available in dye, solvent and pigment varieties. One of my favorite inks is walnut ink, which gives surfaces a vintage, tea-dyed appearance.

PAINTS, DYES AND VARNISHES

The following paints, dyes and varnishes can give a project the ultimate finishing touch. Always use a good-quality paintbrush to apply paints and varnishes to your project surface.

Acrylic paint, readily available in a variety of brands and colors, is fast-drying and can be diluted with water to achieve a watercolor appearance.

Dye, particularly tan Rit dye, can be used to give fabric an "aged" appearance. It works well on wood and heavyweight paper. Rit dye is available at craft, hardware and grocery stores.

Varnishes, which are available in brush-on and spray forms, seal and protect a surface. Varnish can be found in a variety of finishes, including matte, gloss and satin. It is typically applied as the last step of a project. When using spray varnish, use in a well-ventilated area.

Antique varnishes are special varnishes that are tinged brown. In addition to sealing your project, they create an "aged" appearance. These varnishes can be applied to many surfaces, including wood and paper.

ADHESIVES

There is a wide selection of adhesives currently on the market. Familiarize yourself with the options I've described here, and get to know which adhesive works best with which project surfaces. Keep in mind that, when adhering paper and fabric to a surface, a brayer is an excellent tool for burnishing, smoothing and eliminating bubbles.

Paper glue is specially formulated not to wrinkle paper. It is permanent and acid- and lignin-free, which will help your projects last longer. Paper glue, which dries clear, can be rubbed off after drying if needed.

Industrial-strength glue, such as E-6000, is a good choice for attaching buttons and other embellishments.

Fabric glue is permanent and dries crystal clear. This fast-drying glue is ideal for applying lace, ribbon and other trim to project surfaces.

Spray adhesives dry clear and offer an invisible hold. Always use spray adhesives in a well-ventilated area or outside.

Fabric basting glue is used to hold paper or fabric in place while machine stitching or sewing.

Laminating or decoupage medium can be used to adhere both paper and fabric to a project.

A hot glue gun provides an instant bond between lightweight materials.

Fusible web is a thin, peel-away film that, when ironed to a surface, creates a strong adhesive backing. There are different kinds of fusible web; the projects in this book use double-sided fusible web. When machine stitching, make sure the web is suitable for sewing machines; otherwise, it will gum up the needle.

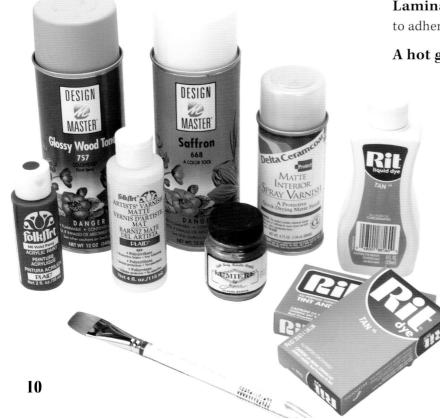

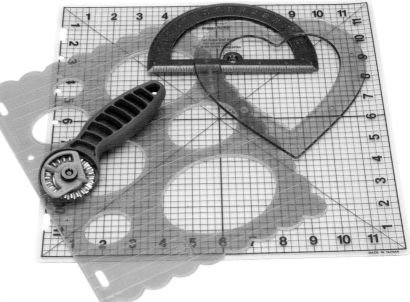

CUTTING AND MEASURING TOOLS

When working with sewing-related projects, your cutting and measuring tools should always be close at hand. The following tools can be purchased at craft, scrapbook and fabric stores.

Scissors are available in straight-edge and decorative-edge varieties. Invest in sturdy scissors that make a nice, clean cut, and, to preserve the scissors' sharpness, dedicate one pair to fabric only and another pair to paper (or paper/fabric) projects. Teflon scissors are excellent when cutting through glued projects, as the glue will not stick to the Teflon finish.

Rotary cutters, which are also available with straight and decorative blades, make cutting paper and fabric very easy. Again, when possible, dedicate one blade to paper and another to fabric. When using a rotary cutter, work on a self-healing mat.

A hot knife/iron is an excellent tool for cutting foamcore board, and it is super easy to use. The trowel point is also very handy for ironing small items.

Plastic templates facilitate the cutting of squares, circles, ovals and many other shapes.

Rulers are available in metal, which is ideal for paper and fabric projects, and plastic, which is preferable when using rotary cutters.

SEWING TOOLS

Last but not least are the sewing tools that you'll need for the "sew easy" projects! For the best selection, check out fabric stores and sewing machine suppliers.

A sewing machine, even the most basic model, is equipped with zig-zag and straight stitches. You'll be using these stitches for several projects. Any sewing machine that is used for fabric can also be used to stitch on paper. I recommend using a sewing machine needle size between 11 and 14 when sewing paper or when sewing paper and fabric together. Some craft stores sell small paper sewing machines in their scrapbook departments.

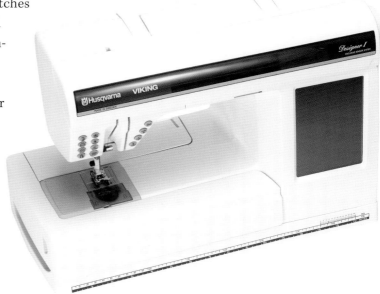

Needles/T-pins can be found in the notion departments of craft and fabric stores. Embroidery needles, which are labelled as such on the packaging, are appropriate for the projects in this book. T-pins are sturdy pins that I use in this book for poking evenly spaced holes before embroidering.

Techniques

You do not have to be a seamstress to make the projects in this book. In fact, the projects use very basic techniques that are easy to learn and master, even if you are a beginner. Whether you are working with paper or fabric, you'll find the techniques described in this section very helpful. If these techniques are new to you, remember that a little bit of practice goes a long way.

SEWING WITH A SEWING MACHINE

If you have never worked a sewing machine in your life, fear not—this is the perfect place to begin. Sewing by machine is fast, easy and, once you learn the basics, addictive! Machines, which vary by manufacturer, are available with a wide variety of features. These days, you can find every model from the simple to the highly sophisticated. For the projects in this book, you need only a basic machine that makes straight and zig-zag stitches.

All modern sewing machines generally operate the same way, and all machines come with a helpful instruction manual. Take the time to acquaint yourself with this manual, then experiment with the machine and its various stitches. Some manufacturers offer online support, and many stores and dealers that sell sewing machines are also very helpful.

Practice on fabric and paper, and, most of all, don't worry about stitches being flawless and perfectly straight. Also, practice with stitch length to determine what offers the most appealing look for your project. A general stitch length is 10–12 stitches per 1" (3cm). When starting a new line of stitching, it is best to backstitch at the beginning and end of each row. This will anchor the stitches so they will not come out. To backstitch, just stitch in a forward direction, then press the backstitch button (or icon) to stitch backward.

JUST SEW YOU KNOW: STITCHING ON PAPER

When machine stitching on paper, be sure to change the needle often, as paper dulls the needle more quickly than fabric. Use the smallest needle possible to prevent making large (and therefore more noticeable) holes in the paper.

STRAIGHT STITCH

The straight stitch is the mainstay of machine stitching. Set your machine to the straight stitch, then align the paper or fabric on the sewing machine bed. Lower the presser foot, press the foot petal, and guide your fabric or paper through.

The zig-zag stitch is a decorative stitch that consists of connected Zs. This stitch is made the same way as the straight stitch—just make sure your machine is set to the zig-zag stitch before you begin.

ZIG-ZAG STITCH

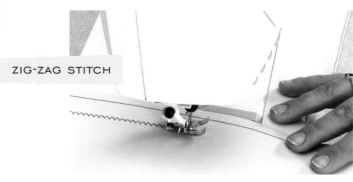

HANDSTITCHING AND HAND EMBROIDERY

If a sewing machine is just not an option for you, keep in mind that all the projects created in this book can also be completed by handstitching or embroidery. Hand embroidery has long been used to decorate clothing and home furnishings—so why not paper? With the popularity of papercrafts, hand embroidery is an excellent option for embellishing paper. You may wonder what the difference is between handstitching and embroidery. Handstitching refers to the more utilitarian stitching used for practical construction of a project, such as sewing a button to fabric. Embroidery refers to decorative stitching and adds a design to a project.

The two essential stitches to know are the running stitch and the backstitch. There are other embroidery stitches that work well on paper, such as French knots, lazy daisy and chain stitches, but I recommend mastering these two stitches first. Once you learn them, you will have a solid foundation for learning the more complicated stitches. I normally use embroidery floss for my handsewn projects, but you can also use silk ribbon, thin ribbon, yarn and other fibers. If desired, beads can be incorporated into embroidery as additional enhancements.

Making a Running Stitch

A running stitch is extremely simple. It allows equal amounts of fabric and stitches to show on the front and back of the material. Often, it is used to baste two materials together. In the demonstration below, I've used it simply as a decorative element.

Sewing Embellishments

When handstitching a button or other embellishment in place, use button or craft thread for extra security. Cut a single strand approximately 18" (46cm) long, then thread it through the appropriate needle and knot one end. When finished sewing, backstitch a couple times through the fabric or paper surface. Knot off the end and trim any excess thread.

1 POKE HOLES

Place the paper on a piece of foamcore board. Then, use a T-pin to poke a line of evenly spaced holes where desired.

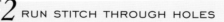

2 RUN STITCH THROUGH HOLES

Thread the embroidery floss, ribbon or other fiber onto a needle, then tie a knot at the end of the tail. Run the needle from back to front through the last hole on one end. Pull taut until the knot catches; if desired, secure the ribbon to the wrong side of the paper with clear tape. Make a running stitch through the holes, running the ribbon through one hole and out the next. Continue until you reach the last hole. Pull the ribbon through to the wrong side and anchor in place with tape or a knot.

Making a Backstitch

The backstitch creates a continuous row of overlapping stitches. This stitch is ideal for outlining a design. For the best results, keep your stitches straight and even—something that is easy to do with practice.

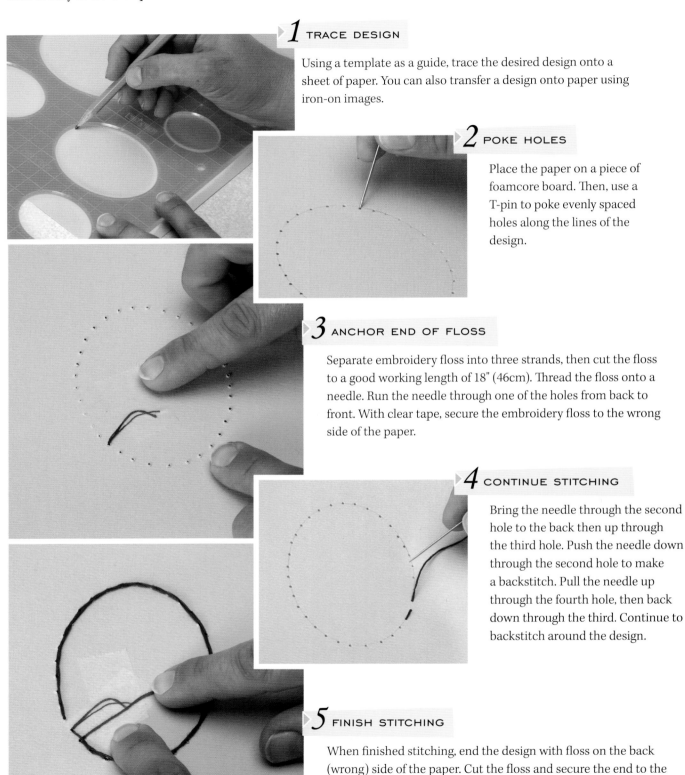

1 TRACE DESIGN

Using a template as a guide, trace the desired design onto a sheet of paper. You can also transfer a design onto paper using iron-on images.

2 POKE HOLES

Place the paper on a piece of foamcore board. Then, use a T-pin to poke evenly spaced holes along the lines of the design.

3 ANCHOR END OF FLOSS

Separate embroidery floss into three strands, then cut the floss to a good working length of 18" (46cm). Thread the floss onto a needle. Run the needle through one of the holes from back to front. With clear tape, secure the embroidery floss to the wrong side of the paper.

4 CONTINUE STITCHING

Bring the needle through the second hole to the back then up through the third hole. Push the needle down through the second hole to make a backstitch. Pull the needle up through the fourth hole, then back down through the third. Continue to backstitch around the design.

5 FINISH STITCHING

When finished stitching, end the design with floss on the back (wrong) side of the paper. Cut the floss and secure the end to the paper with clear tape.

Using Fusible Web

As one of my staple supplies, fusible web is used in several projects in this book. In some cases, you can substitute glue or double-sided tape for fusible web, but I recommend using it whenever possible. It guarantees great results!

1 CUT FUSIBLE WEB AND MATERIAL

Cut a piece of fabric or paper, then cut a piece of fusible web to approximately the same size.

2 PEEL OFF CARRIER SHEET

Peel the carrier sheet off one side of the fusible web. This will expose a sticky surface.

3 FUSE WEB TO MATERIAL

Place the sticky side of the fusible web on the fabric. (Unless otherwise instructed, apply the web to the wrong side of the fabric.) Run an iron over the fusible web or fabric to fuse the two surfaces together.

NOTE: *Follow the manufacturer's instructions to determine the proper heat setting of the iron.*

4 PEEL AWAY CARRIER SHEET

Once the two surfaces are fused, there will be a carrier sheet lining one side of the material. Peel the carrier sheet from the material to expose the sticky surface.

5 FUSE MATERIAL TO BASE SURFACE

Place the sticky side on your base surface, such as a piece of cardstock. Run an iron over the fabric or cardstock to fuse the two surfaces together.

6 ADD LAYERS, IF DESIRED

If desired, you can overlap another piece of fusible web-backed fabric right on top, repeating steps 1 to 5. If you are adding layers, double-sided fusible web is ideal, as you can "audition" the pieces by placing and then repositioning them before permanently fusing them with an iron.

CARDS AND STATIONERY

Handmade cards and stationery offer a great opportunity for trying your hand at new techniques and styles. If you are a sewing novice, relax your perfectionist tendencies and give yourself plenty of time to play around with different looks. In shedding the expectation to be perfect, you'll find the freedom to discover "sew many" possibilities! Whether you incorporate hand embroidery, machine stitching or just some simple sewing notions, you can give your cards almost any look—warm and casual, elegant and sophisticated, hip and edgy, nostalgic and retro, classic and vintage.

Your handmade cards will be so much more appealing and more heartfelt than any store-bought card. And keep in mind that these cards can be more than just an accessory to a gift—they can be the gift itself! Make several notecards, then make custom envelopes to match. Tie the stationery in a bundle with a length of pretty ribbon, lace or raffia. You'll have a great gift for any occasion!

IF YOU'VE HAD LITTLE OR NO EXPERIENCE sewing, this card is a great place to start. The simple handstitching technique used to embellish the card couldn't be easier to learn, and it always yields gorgeous results. Once you master this technique, you've opened the door to all kinds of crafting possibilities. For this birthday card, I embroidered cardstock with silk ribbon, giving the design a touch of elegance to complement the refined style of the decorative paper.

MATERIALS AND TOOLS

IMAGE FOR CARD

SOLID-COLOR CARDSTOCK (TWO COLORS)

DECORATIVE CARDSTOCK

DECORATIVE TEXT-WEIGHT PAPER

FOAMCORE BOARD

SILK RIBBON

EMBROIDERY NEEDLE

T-PIN

SCISSORS

SCALLOP SHEARS

PAPER GLUE

CLEAR TAPE

LOVING BIRTHDAY WISHES
(OR GREETING OF YOUR CHOICE) RUBBER STAMP

INK PAD

1 FOLD AND TRIM CARD

Fold a piece of cardstock to make a card that opens from the side. Trim the card's front panel in half, then trim again to give the top a rounded shape. Trim the back panel to give it a rounded shape as well. Trim the rounded edge of the front of the card with scallop shears.

2 ADD IMAGE

Print or copy the image of your choice onto a sheet of cream cardstock. (I used a Vintage Workshop CD-ROM and printed the image from my computer.) Trim the image to fit on the front panel of the card. Use paper glue to glue it just below the scallop edge.

19

3 POKE HOLES

Open the card and place it on a piece of foam-core board. Use a T-pin to poke evenly spaced holes along the top edge of the front panel.

4 EMBROIDER FRONT PANEL

Thread a length of silk ribbon onto an embroidery needle. Make a running stitch through the holes, anchoring each end of the ribbon with clear tape on the back of the panel (see Making a Running Stitch, page 13).

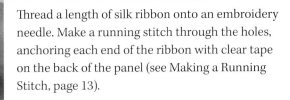

5 MAKE GREETING TAG

Stamp a greeting of your choice onto a piece of cardstock. Trim the greeting, then use paper glue to mount it onto one or more pieces of solid and decorative cardstock to give the tag a framed look. Use a T-pin to poke a hole on either side of the stamped greeting, and tie a little French knot through each hole (see Knot Too Hard At All, on page 21).

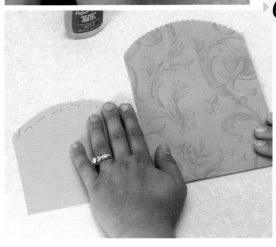

6 LINE BACK PANEL

Cut a piece of decorative paper to cover the back panel of the card. Adhere the paper liner to the back panel with paper glue. Cut the top edge of the back panel into a rounded shape with scallop shears to match the front panel.

7 ATTACH TAG TO BACK PANEL

Glue the greeting tag to the back panel of the card, as shown.

Knot Too Hard at All

It's not difficult to make a French knot. To begin, thread a piece of ribbon onto an embroidery needle. (1) First, bring the ribbon through the hole. (2) Wrap the ribbon counter-clockwise three times around the needle. (3) Bring the needle back through the hole. Pull the ribbon taut and anchor it in place with tape.

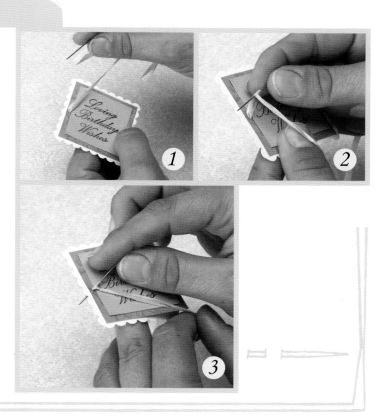

Initial Correspondence

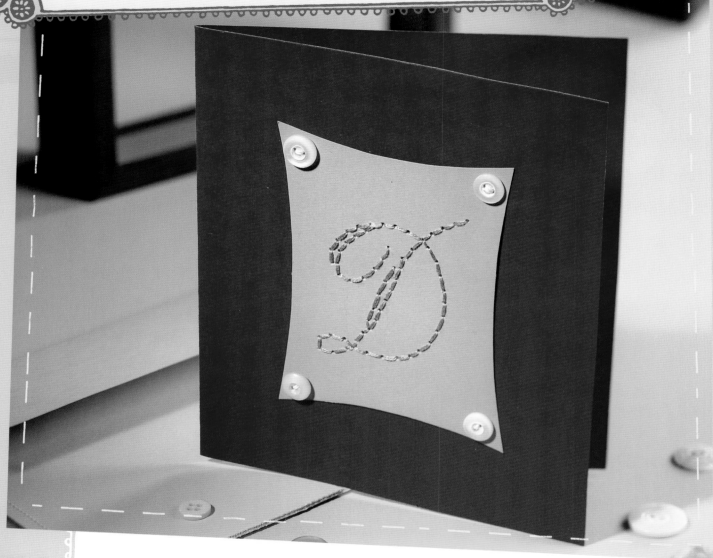

WHAT WILL YOUR FRIEND'S "INITIAL" THOUGHTS be when she sees this card, embellished with her very own initials? No doubt, she'll be impressed! Simple, classic and versatile, monograms are the perfect embellishment. By personalizing a design with the recipient's initials, you can dress up any project while creating a truly tailored look. It's not difficult; for this card, I transferred a simple iron-on monogram onto cardstock, then embroidered the monogram for a fantastic look.

MATERIALS AND TOOLS

SOLID-COLOR CARDSTOCK (TWO COLORS)

FOAMCORE BOARD

HOT-IRON TRANSFER MONOGRAM

SIX-STRAND EMBROIDERY FLOSS

BUTTON THREAD

NEEDLE

EMBROIDERY NEEDLE

T-PIN

SCISSORS

PAPER GLUE

CLEAR TAPE

BUTTONS

HOT TOOL OR IRON

For the Envelope:

SOLID-COLOR CARDSTOCK

SCISSORS (OR DECORATIVE-EDGE SCISSORS)

SEWING MACHINE AND THREAD

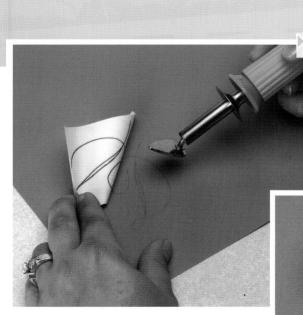

1 TRANSFER LETTER TO PAPER

Tape a hot-iron transfer monogram, image side down, onto a piece of cardstock. Run a hot iron over the transfer paper to transfer the monogram onto the cardstock.

NOTE: *If you prefer, you can lightly draw a monogram directly onto the paper with pencil instead of using the hot-iron transfer paper.*

2 POKE HOLES

Remove the transfer paper, then place the monogrammed cardstock on a piece of foamcore board. Use a T-pin to poke evenly spaced holes along the lines of the monogram.

3 EMBROIDER MONOGRAM

Cut out the monogram, trimming the cardstock to any shape you desire. Using three strands of embroidery floss, embroider the monogram with a backstitch, running the floss through the holes (see Making a Backstitch, page 14). Before beginning and after finishing the embroidery, anchor the end of the floss to the back of the cardstock with a small piece of tape.

4 GLUE MONOGRAM TO CARD

Cut and fold another piece of cardstock to make a card. Glue the embroidered monogram to the front of the card with a dab of paper glue.

SEW EASY TIP

Once you finish step 3, you can make a few color copies of the embroidered monogram. A color copy will retain the three-dimensional look of the embroidery, and you can use the monogram as an embellishment for notecards, tags and other stationery.

5 STITCH BUTTONS TO MONOGRAM

Using the button thread and needle, stitch one button in each corner of the embroidered monogram cardstock, bringing the stitch all the way through the front panel of the card and back to secure the monogram in place.

6 ADD BACKING TO CARD INTERIOR

Cut a piece of cardstock to back the inside of the card's front panel. Glue the cardstock to the panel, concealing any stitches.

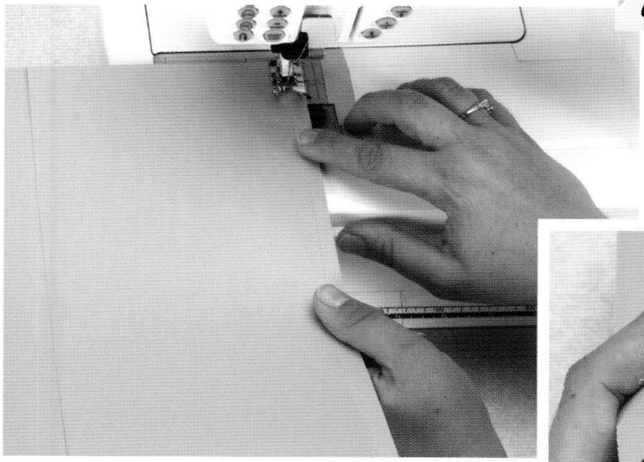

7 PREPARE CARDSTOCK FOR ENVELOPE

Stack two 8½" x 11" (22cm x 28cm) sheets of cardstock. Machine stitch the two sheets together, stitching ¼" (6mm) in from the long edge of the paper.

8 FOLD CARDSTOCK

Fold the cardstock so that the ¼" (6mm) seam is on the inside of the fold. This will be the bottom of the envelope.

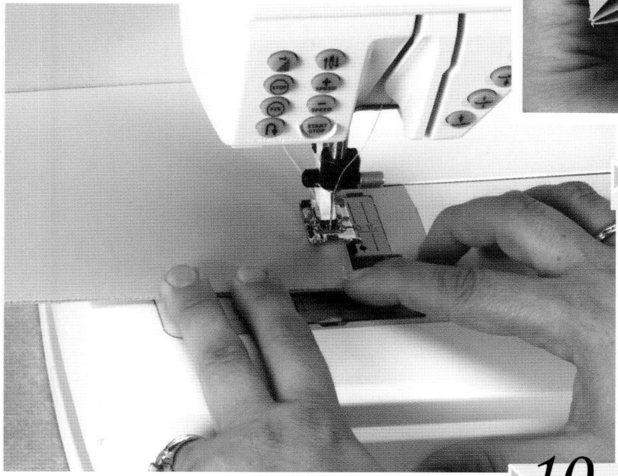

9 TRIM AND STITCH EDGES TO FORM POCKET

Place the card on the envelope to determine where the right and left sides of the envelope should be cut. Trim the sides; you can use decorative-edge scissors for added flair. Then, machine stitch the right and left edges of the envelope to form a pocket.

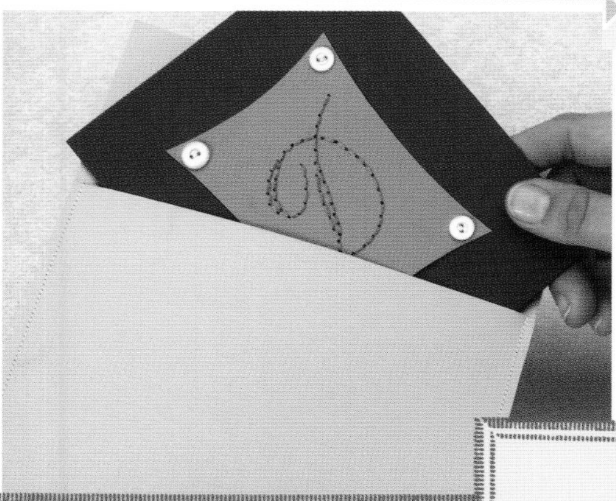

10 INSERT CARD INTO ENVELOPE

When the envelope is finished, insert the card and seal closed with glue, tape or a sticker.

To lengthen or shorten front, back illustration above. Slight changes made at lower edge.

ments issued by of Commerce —

TAILOR YOUR LOOK!

Use a backstitch to embroider any greeting on cardstock. The handcrafted look offers a heart-warming touch.

Thank You

Heart-Felt Hello

THIS IS ANOTHER HANDCRAFTED CARD that incorporates a pretty monogram into the exterior design. Here, the monogram is mounted on a colorful panel constructed from decorative paper strips. The process is easy—just machine stitch several strips of decorative paper together to create one large sheet. The sheet can be cut up and used to embellish a huge batch of beautiful cards. You could even assemble the paper strips to create a coordinating mat for the card. For the card base, I used stiffened felt, a handy material that can be purchased at any craft store.

MATERIALS AND TOOLS

DECORATIVE PAPERS

12" x 12" (30CM X 30CM)
DECORATIVE CARDSTOCK

STIFFENED FELT (AVAILABLE AT CRAFT STORES)

DECORATIVE MONOGRAM (ALPHABET CLIP ART)

SIX-STRAND EMBROIDERY FLOSS

EMBROIDERY NEEDLE

T-PIN

SCISSORS

PINKING SHEARS

PAPER GLUE

FABRIC GLUE

CLEAR TAPE

STAPLER

SLIDE PAPER TRIMMER (OR RULER, PENCIL,
CRAFT KNIFE AND SELF-HEALING CUTTING MAT)

SEWING MACHINE AND THREAD

For the Envelope:

MANILA FILE FOLDER

FOAMCORE BOARD

EMBROIDERY FLOSS

T-PIN

EMBROIDERY NEEDLE

RULER

PENCIL

1 COVER CARDSTOCK WITH PAPER STRIPS

Using a slide paper trimmer or craft knife, cut several strips of decorative paper 1½" (4cm) wide. Line up the strips, edge to edge, on the sheet of decorative cardstock. Staple the strips to keep them in place, then use a sewing machine to zig-zag stitch the strips to the cardstock, stitching right along the edges of the strips.

2 CREATE EMBELLISHMENT FOR CARD

Using pinking shears, cut a 2" x 3¼" (5cm x 8cm) rectangle from the stitched paper. Use regular scissors to cut out a decorative monogram, trimming it to a rectangle smaller than 2" x 3¼" (5cm x 8cm). Glue the monogram onto the stitched rectangle with paper glue.

3 EMBROIDER CORNERS

Use a T-pin to poke four holes in a square formation on each corner of the stitched rectangle. Handstitch an *X* through each set of holes, using six strands of embroidery floss. Anchor the ends of the floss to the back with a small piece of tape.

4 STITCH SPINE OF CARD

Cut and fold a piece of stiffened felt to the desired card size. Cut and fold a sheet of cardstock to a slightly smaller size, then place it inside the felt card. Using a ¼" (6mm) seam allowance, machine stitch along the folded edge of the card, stitching the felt exterior and the cardstock interior together.

5 ADHERE EMBELLISHMENTS

Use fabric glue to adhere the monogram embellishment onto the front of the card.

6 PREPARE ENVELOPE PAPER

Lay an open manila folder (or whatever paper you have chosen for your envelope) on your work surface. Place the card on the folder to determine how large you will need to make the envelope. (The bottom fold of the folder will serve as the bottom fold of the envelope.)

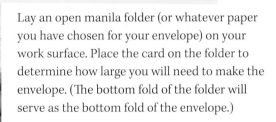

▶ *7* TRIM PAPER

Trim the sides to the make the envelope the correct size. Fold the bottom panel up, then fold the top panel down to make a flap.

▶ *8* POKE HOLES ALONG EDGES

Place the envelope on your work surface with the flap open. Place a ruler parallel to the left edge, ¼" (6mm) from the edge, and run a pencil along the ruler; repeat along the right edge. Place the envelope on a piece of foamcore, then use a T-pin to poke evenly spaced holes along each pencil line. If desired, poke holes through the tab part of the flap as well.

▶ *9* EMBROIDER ENVELOPE

Cut an 18" (46cm) length of embroidery floss, then tie a knot at one end of the floss and thread the other end through a needle. With the embroidery floss, make a whipstitch by bringing the needle down through each hole so that the thread wraps around the edge of the envelope. Whipstitch the remaining edges in the same manner. When finished, place the card in the envelope.

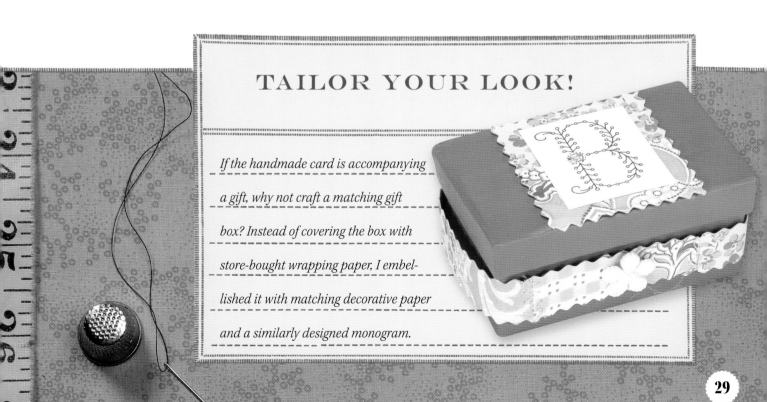

TAILOR YOUR LOOK!

If the handmade card is accompanying

a gift, why not craft a matching gift

box? Instead of covering the box with

store-bought wrapping paper, I embel-

lished it with matching decorative paper

and a similarly designed monogram.

Colorful Greetings

REMEMBER HOW FUN IT WAS TO COLOR with crayons? Go back to your creative roots and rediscover the joy of crayons with this hand-made card. With a little coloring here and a little embroidery there, your card is finished, already matted and ready to be framed. Iron transfers, used in this project for the butterfly design, can be found in the needle-work department of any craft store. Available in a variety of styles and themes, iron transfers come in small paper packages. Traditionally, they have been used as transfers for tea towels and tablecloths, but, as this project demonstrates, they work beautifully on paper, too.

MATERIALS AND TOOLS

SOLID-COLOR CARDSTOCK

12" x 12" (30CM x 30CM)
DECORATIVE CARDSTOCK

SOLID-COLOR COTTON FABRIC

IRON TRANSFER DESIGN

METALLIC EMBROIDERY FLOSS

EMBROIDERY NEEDLE

SCISSORS

CRAFT KNIFE

PAPER GLUE

SPRAY ADHESIVE

SQUARE TEMPLATE

EMBROIDERY HOOP

RULER

WAX CRAYONS

PENCIL OR DISAPPEARING MARKER

HOT TOOL OR IRON

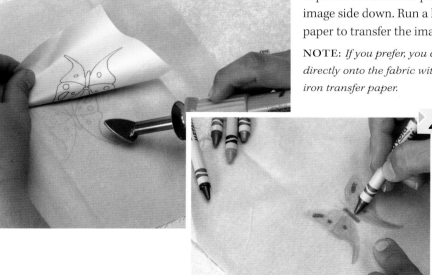

▷1 TRANSFER IMAGE TO FABRIC

Tape the iron transfer paper to the cotton fabric, image side down. Run a hot iron over the transfer paper to transfer the image to the fabric.

NOTE: *If you prefer, you can lightly draw an image directly onto the fabric with pencil instead of using the iron transfer paper.*

▷2 COLOR IMAGE

Apply color to the image with wax crayons.

3 SET THE COLOR WITH HEAT

Run a hot iron directly over the image to set the color.

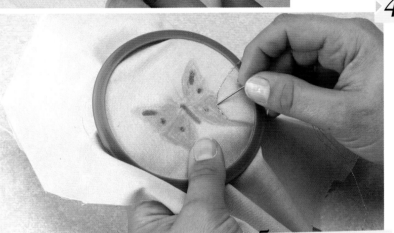

4 EMBROIDER IMAGE

Place the image in an embroidery hoop. Embroider the lines of the image with a backstitch, using two strands of metallic floss and the embroidery needle (see Making a Backstitch, page 14).

5 PREPARE CARD

Fold the 12" x 12" (30cm x 30cm) sheet of decorative cardstock into quarters to make a card. Unfold the card, then use a template and pencil or disappearing marker to trace a square onto the quarter that will be the front panel of the card. The square should be centered on the panel, and it should be large enough to accommodate the image. Cut out the window with a craft knife.

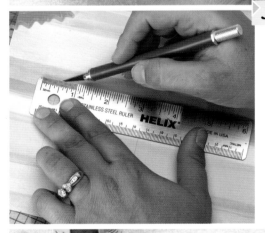

6 MOUNT CARDSTOCK TO IMAGE

If necessary, trim the fabric so that it will fit behind the front panel; be sure to make it a little larger than the window. Cut a piece of cardstock to the same size as the fabric. Place the fabric, image side down, on your work surface. Spray the back of the fabric with adhesive, then adhere the cardstock.

7 GLUE IMAGE IN WINDOW

Hold the cardstock-backed image in the window, positioning as desired. After determining the proper placement, secure it to the paper with paper glue.

8 FINISH CARD

Refold the card, then adhere the corners together with a dab of paper glue.

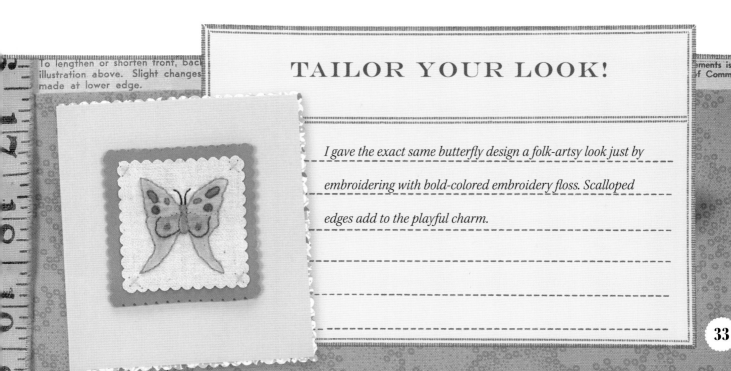

To lengthen or shorten front, back illustration above. Slight changes made at lower edge.

TAILOR YOUR LOOK!

I gave the exact same butterfly design a folk-artsy look just by embroidering with bold-colored embroidery floss. Scalloped edges add to the playful charm.

Dress-Up Card

THIS CHIC GREETING CARD IS SASSY, SIMPLE and stylish. You don't need to be a fashion guru to dress this project up to the nines; you need only a scrap of lace and some felt. If you have some fancy buttons or beads on hand, use them to accessorize the "outfit." With just a few changes, you can customize the look to fit the personality of the recipient—a die-hard shopper, a trendy fashionista, a decked-out diva, a radiant bride-to-be or just a favorite girlfriend. For a special gift, make several cards with all different "dress-up" looks and package them together as a set of all-occasion stationery.

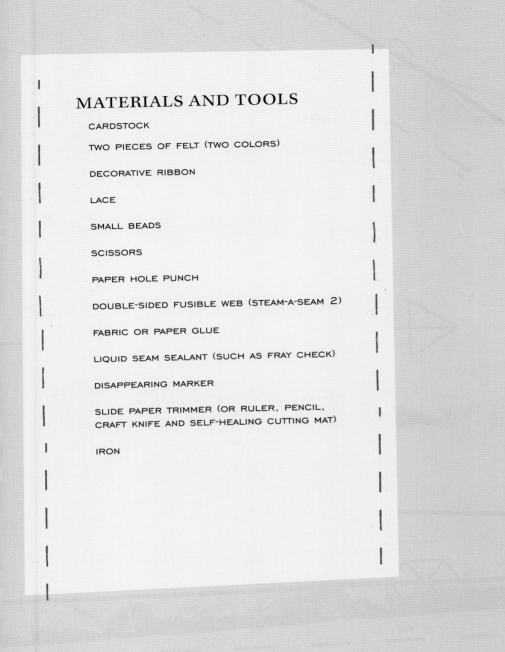

MATERIALS AND TOOLS

CARDSTOCK

TWO PIECES OF FELT (TWO COLORS)

DECORATIVE RIBBON

LACE

SMALL BEADS

SCISSORS

PAPER HOLE PUNCH

DOUBLE-SIDED FUSIBLE WEB (STEAM-A-SEAM 2)

FABRIC OR PAPER GLUE

LIQUID SEAM SEALANT (SUCH AS FRAY CHECK)

DISAPPEARING MARKER

SLIDE PAPER TRIMMER (OR RULER, PENCIL, CRAFT KNIFE AND SELF-HEALING CUTTING MAT)

IRON

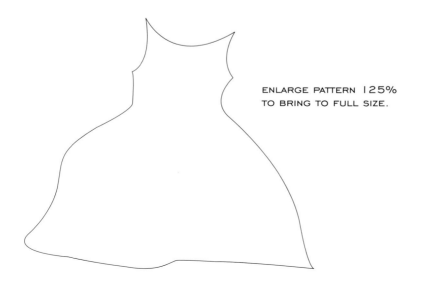

ENLARGE PATTERN 125%
TO BRING TO FULL SIZE.

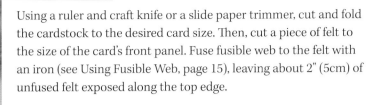

1 FUSE FELT

Using a ruler and craft knife or a slide paper trimmer, cut and fold the cardstock to the desired card size. Then, cut a piece of felt to the size of the card's front panel. Fuse fusible web to the felt with an iron (see Using Fusible Web, page 15), leaving about 2" (5cm) of unfused felt exposed along the top edge.

2 FUSE LACE TO FELT

Peel the carrier sheet off the felt. Place a piece of lace on the sticky surface of the felt, then run an iron over the lace to fuse it in place.

3 TRACE DRESS ONTO FELT

Use a disappearing marker to trace the dress pattern over the felt, lining up the pattern so that the edge of the lace corresponds with the dress waistline.

4 ADHERE DRESS TO CARD

Cut out the dress and glue it to the front of the card with fabric or paper glue.

5 ADD FELT DOTS

Punch dots out of both colors of felt with a hole punch. Glue the dots to the front of the card in a decorative pattern.

6 PUNCH HOLES IN CARD

Use a paper punch to make two holes on the front of the card, placing them at the top center.

7 MAKE BOW

Run each end of the ribbon through the holes and tie a bow. Put liquid seam sealant on the ends of the ribbon so they don't fray.

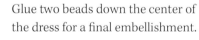

8 FINISH CARD

Glue two beads down the center of the dress for a final embellishment.

Card-in-a-Pocket

FABRIC PAPER AND CARDSTOCK TEAM up to create this playful card, and simple machine stitching brings the two materials together, giving the card a finished look. I decided to use a fun retro floral theme, but, with so many exciting fabric patterns and paper designs out there, you can mix and match your own combination. Use the pocket to hold a special note of congratulations, a wish for happiness or just a simple hello. The finished product is uniquely charming, and it's sure to draw rave reviews from the recipient!

MATERIALS AND TOOLS

TWO SHEETS SOLID-COLOR CARDSTOCK
(GREEN, BURGUNDY)

FABRIC PAPER WITH COORDINATING PATTERNS
(PURPLE, GREEN AND RED FLORAL)

PIN OR TACK

SCISSORS

SCALLOP SHEARS

PAPER GLUE

CONGRATULATIONS (OR GREETING OF
YOUR CHOICE) RUBBER STAMP

INK PAD

BRADS

CLIP BRAD

SLIDE PAPER TRIMMER (OR RULER, PENCIL,
CRAFT KNIFE AND SELF-HEALING CUTTING MAT)

RULER

SEWING MACHINE AND THREAD

1 PREPARE CARD BASE

Using a ruler and craft knife or a slide paper trimmer,
cut a 5½" x 8¼" (14cm x 21cm) piece of cardstock.
Measure down 3" (8cm) from the top edge and fold
down, as shown, to make a flap. Trim the flap edge
with scallop shears.

2 ADD FABRIC TO FLAP

Cut a 2¼" x 4½" (6cm x 11cm)
piece of fabric paper to fit on
the flap of the base cardstock.
Machine stitch the fabric paper
onto the flap.

3 CUT CARDSTOCK AND FABRIC

Cut a 4¾" x 5" (12cm x 13cm) piece of cardstock with scissors and a 4½" x 4¾" (11cm x 12cm) piece of fabric paper with scallop shears.

4 STITCH TOGETHER

Machine stitch the fabric paper square onto the cardstock.

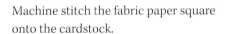

5 PLACE BRAD IN CENTER

Use a ruler to determine the center of the stitched fabric paper square, then use a pin or tack to poke a hole through the center point. Insert and secure a clip brad through the hole.

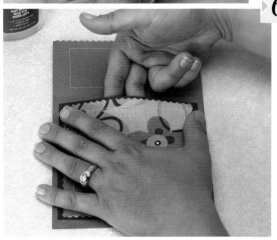

6 ATTACH POCKET

Turn the stitched fabric square over and apply a line of glue around three edges, leaving the top edge unglued. Lift the flap of the card and adhere the square onto the base cardstock so that it forms a pocket.

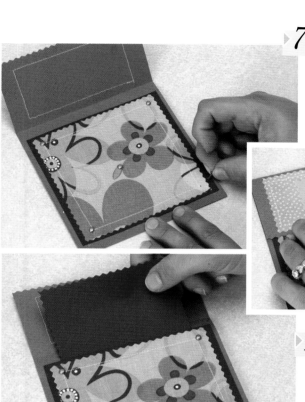

▶ **7** ADD BRADS

Poke a hole through each corner of the stitched square and secure a brad through each hole.

▶ **8** ADD GREETING TO FLAP

Stamp a greeting of your choice on a piece of cardstock. Trim the cardstock to 2½" x 1½" (6cm x 4cm) using scallop shears. Glue the greeting onto the flap, directly on top of the fabric.

▶ **9** ADD NOTECARD

Cut a 3¾" x 4¾" (9cm x 12cm) piece of cardstock to fit inside the pocket. Personalize the notecard with a message, then slip it into the pocket.

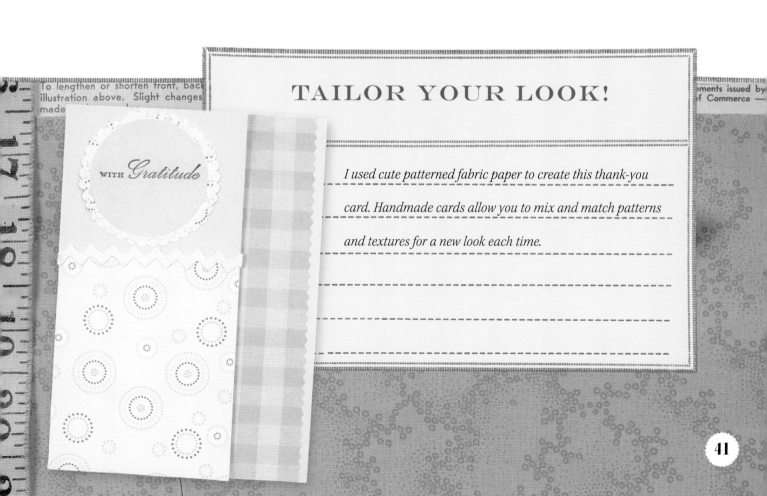

TAILOR YOUR LOOK!

WITH *Gratitude*

I used cute patterned fabric paper to create this thank-you card. Handmade cards allow you to mix and match patterns and textures for a new look each time.

Fancy Ruffled Card

THIS CARD FEATURES A DECORATIVE RUFFLE, which provides a fancy frame for the "Best Wishes" greeting. Don't worry—"fancy" doesn't have to mean "complicated." In fact, it's quite easy to make the ruffle embellishment, and once you learn the technique, you can use it over and over. The ruffle offers a versatile look, which makes it an ideal design element for a variety of styles, from old-fashioned to whimsical. With such a unique touch, your cards will be as much fun to give as they are to make!

MATERIALS AND TOOLS

SOLID-COLOR CARDSTOCK (CREAM)

TWO PIECES OF FABRIC WITH COORDINATING
PATTERNS (RED, PINK AND CREAM FLORAL;
RED AND YELLOW POLKA DOT)

CHIPBOARD

RIBBON

BUTTON THREAD

NEEDLE

SCISSORS

SCALLOP SHEARS

DOUBLE-SIDED FUSIBLE WEB (STEAM-A-SEAM 2)

FABRIC GLUE

BEST WISHES (OR GREETING OF YOUR CHOICE)
RUBBER STAMP

INK PAD

MINIATURE DECORATIVE METAL FRAME

RULER

DISAPPEARING MARKER

SLIDE PAPER TRIMMER (OR RULER, PENCIL,
CRAFT KNIFE AND SELF-HEALING CUTTING MAT)

IRON

1 PREPARE CARDSTOCK AND FABRIC

Using a ruler and craft knife or a slide paper trimmer, cut a
piece of cardstock to use for your notecard. Cut a piece of
fabric large enough to cover the card, then fuse it to a sheet of
fusible web with a warm iron (see Using Fusible Web, page 15).

2 COVER AND TRIM CARDSTOCK

Fuse the fabric to the cardstock.
Trim the edges of the cardstock
with scallop shears.

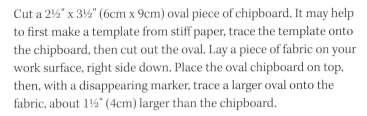

3 CUT OUT FABRIC OVAL

Cut a 2½" x 3½" (6cm x 9cm) oval piece of chipboard. It may help to first make a template from stiff paper, trace the template onto the chipboard, then cut out the oval. Lay a piece of fabric on your work surface, right side down. Place the oval chipboard on top, then, with a disappearing marker, trace a larger oval onto the fabric, about 1½" (4cm) larger than the chipboard.

4 RUN STITCH AROUND FABRIC OVAL

Using button thread and a needle, make a running stitch around the edge of the fabric oval (see Making a Running Stitch, page 13). When finished, leave the thread on the needle; do not cut or knot the thread.

5 MAKE RUFFLE

Place the fabric oval on your work surface, right side down, and then place the chipboard oval on top, centered on the fabric. Pull the thread so that the fabric gathers and closes tightly around the oval. Run a couple of stitches through the fabric opening, then knot the thread and trim it.

6 STAMP GREETING

Stamp a piece of cardstock with a desired greeting.

▶ 7 FRAME GREETING

Glue a miniature decorative frame over the greeting, then trim the excess paper around the frame.

▶ 8 GLUE GREETING TO OVAL

Glue the framed greeting to the fabric oval, centering it before adhering it with fabric glue.

▶ 9 FINISH CARD

Glue the fabric oval to the front of the card with fabric glue. Cut a length of ribbon and tie it in a bow, then glue it onto the card, just below the fabric oval.

TAILOR YOUR LOOK!

Here I made a smaller ruffle from scrap fabric, then used a paper frame to highlight it as the card's central decorative feature.

BOXES, TINS AND POUCHES

For something a little different, think outside the box—or maybe inside the box! This section focuses on special places to store personal keepsakes. Why shouldn't the exterior of a container be as impressive as, or more impressive than, its contents? And why should you bother wrapping a gift, when you can make the gift box itself a treasure? You might be surprised how just a little fabric, some ribbon and a few stitches can make a plain old container spectacular!

Some of these projects incorporate store-bought containers, such as wooden and papier-mâché boxes. These are like prefabricated blank canvases, with surfaces that are ready to be decorated. Other containers are waiting to be discovered in the most unexpected places. Who would've guessed you could recycle old mint tins or crocheted potholders in such a unique way!

Crepe-Over-Tin Case

THIS SIMPLE PROJECT OFFERS ALL THE CHARM of a handmade gift but requires so little time. In fact, it takes only minutes to transform a standard tin case into a mini-masterpiece! Decorative paper gives the case a little personality, and crepe fabric adds an elegant, luminous touch. To turn the project into a complete gift package, create a set of handmade stationery to match the case design. The finished product is sure to impress—and nobody ever needs to know how easy it was to make!

MATERIALS AND TOOLS

TIN CASE

DECORATIVE PAPER

SOLID-COLOR CARDSTOCK

CREPE FABRIC

SCISSORS

DOUBLE-SIDED FUSIBLE WEB (STEAM-A-SEAM 2)

PAPER GLUE

PENCIL

IRON

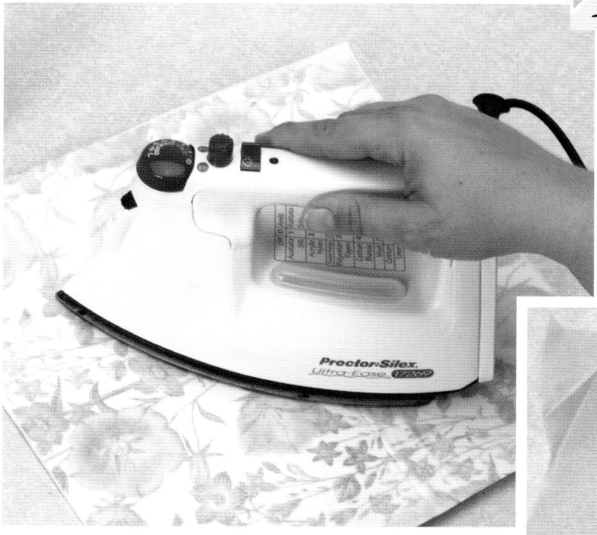

1 PREPARE PAPER WITH FUSIBLE WEB

Cut one sheet of fusible web and one sheet of decorative paper, each sheet large enough to cover both sides of the tin case. Peel the carrier sheet off one side of the fusible web, then adhere it to the right side (front) of the decorative paper. Iron the fusible web onto the paper.

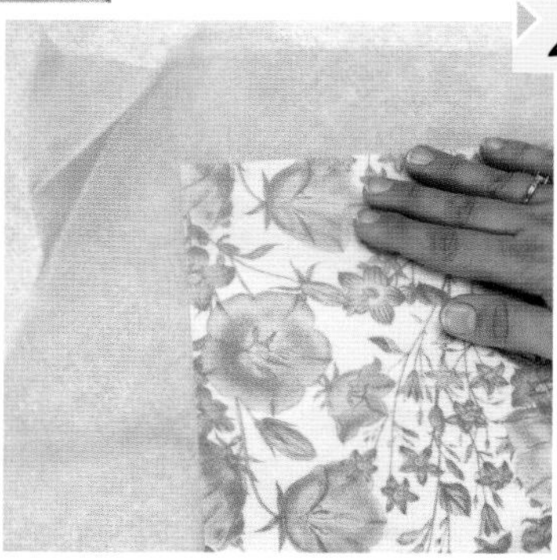

2 ADHERE CREPE TO PAPER

Peel the carrier sheet off the decorative paper to expose the sticky surface. Press a piece of sheer crepe fabric onto the sticky surface and smooth it down with your hands.

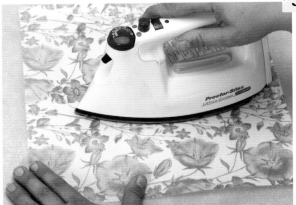

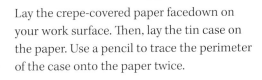

▸ 3 IRON CREPE

Run a warm iron over the crepe-covered paper.

▸ 4 TRACE AROUND CASE

Lay the crepe-covered paper facedown on your work surface. Then, lay the tin case on the paper. Use a pencil to trace the perimeter of the case onto the paper twice.

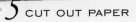

▸ 5 CUT OUT PAPER

Cut out the paper, trimming along the traced lines to create a front cover and a back cover for the case.

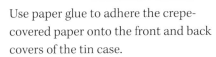

▸ 6 ADHERE PAPER TO CASE

Use paper glue to adhere the crepe-covered paper onto the front and back covers of the tin case.

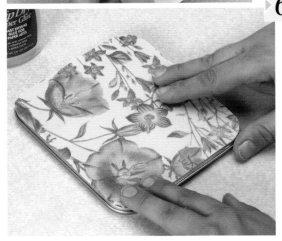

7 CREATE STATIONERY

Using scraps of the crepe-covered paper, make corresponding stationery and notecards from cardstock to fit inside the case. When finished, place the stationery in the case.

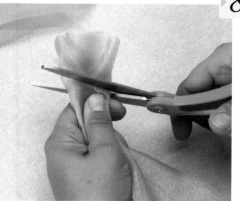

8 CUT RIBBON

Fold or roll the crepe fabric several times, then cut the end to make a ribbon. Do not worry about cutting a straight edge; the uneven edge will give the ribbon an interesting look.

9 TIE BOW

Tie the crepe ribbon around the tin case and finish with a bow.

SEW EASY TIP

Instead of using crepe fabric, like I did in this project, try using organza or tulle. You can preview the effect you'll get simply by placing the fabric over your paper.

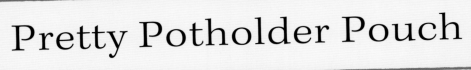

Pretty Potholder Pouch

ABUNDANT AT FLEA MARKET AND TAG SALES, crocheted potholders are inexpensive but priceless little gems. I am eager to purchase
them, knowing that vintage potholders never cease to generate new ideas
for projects. Whenever I see them for sale, it always amazes me that the
fruits of somebody's hard work and creative spirit can be bought for just
pennies. I like to take inspiration from that creative spirit, and pick up
where the creator left off. You never know what kinds of unexpected uses
you'll come up with! Here, I sew two together, creating a cute pouch for a
hand-decorated journal.

MATERIALS AND TOOLS

TWO MATCHING CROCHETED POTHOLDERS

SMALL COMPOSITION BOOK

DECORATIVE PAPER

GROSGRAIN RIBBON (FOR BOW)

THREAD

NEEDLE

SCISSORS

HOT GLUE GUN

BASTING GLUE

DECORATIVE METAL LETTER

PENCIL

SEWING MACHINE

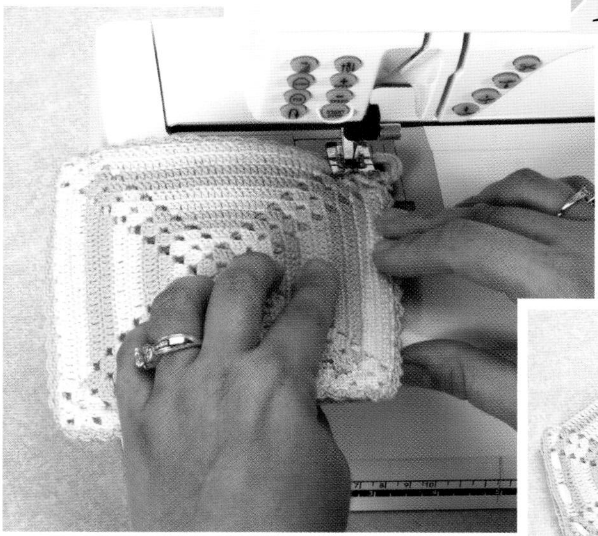

1 STITCH POTHOLDERS TOGETHER

Machine stitch two identical potholders together, joining three sides to form a pocket (see Sew Easy Tip, at right).

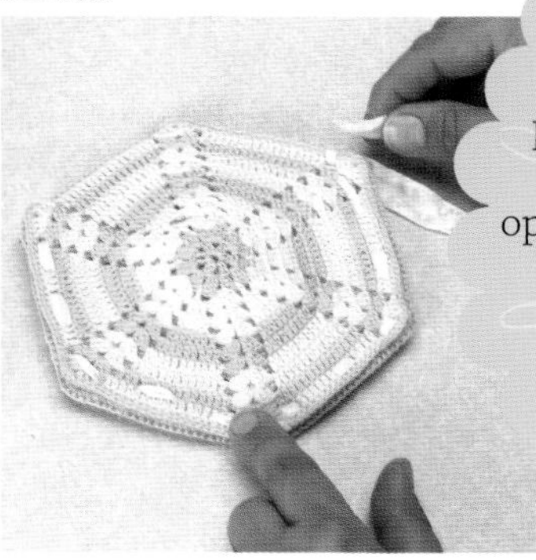

SEW EASY TIP

Machine stitching is not your only option for joining the two potholders: you can simply handstitch them with thread or even ribbon, as shown here.

53

2 ADD BOW

Tie the grosgrain ribbon into a small decorative bow. Hot glue the bow onto the front top of the pocket.

3 ADD MORE EMBELLISHMENTS

Sew additional embellishments onto the front as desired, such as a decorative letter, as shown here.

4 PREPARE PAPER FOR JOURNAL COVER

Lay a sheet of decorative paper facedown on your work surface. Place the small composition book on the paper, then trace around the perimeter of the front and back covers.

5 ADHERE PAPER TO COVERS

Cut the paper, following along the traced lines. Trim the paper to fit on the front and back covers of the book, then use basting glue to adhere the paper to the covers.

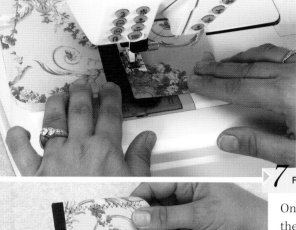

▶6 ADD DECORATIVE STITCHING TO JOURNAL

Using a sewing machine, add a decorative straight or zig-zag stitch to the book's front and back covers.

▶7 PLACE JOURNAL IN POCKET

Once the journal is finished, place it in the crocheted purse pocket.

To lengthen or shorten front, back
illustration above. Slight changes
made at lower edge.

ments issued by
of Commerce —

TAILOR YOUR LOOK!

Here, I cut several sheets of paper a little smaller than the

crocheted potholders, then stacked the paper between

the two potholders. I stitched the paper and potholders

together along the left side to create a little booklet with

crocheted covers.

Fabulous Fabric Boxes

"PRESENTATION IS EVERYTHING," as the saying goes. Nothing makes a more beautiful presentation than these fabric-covered boxes. When adorned with coordinating patterns and colors, the boxes are transformed from simple containers to magnificent works of art. These can be used to hold gifts, or they can function as lovely accents for the home. Consider keeping papier-mâché boxes as a staple in your stash of crafting supplies. That way, in a pinch, you can quickly cover a box for an extra-fancy gift presentation.

MATERIALS AND TOOLS

PAPIER-MÂCHÉ BOXES
(SET OF THREE, IF DESIRED)

CARDSTOCK

FABRIC (IN THREE COORDINATING PATTERNS,
IF DESIRED)

RIBBON (COORDINATING WITH FABRIC)

SCISSORS

FABRIC GLUE

LIQUID SEAM SEALANT (SUCH AS FRAY CHECK)

HOLE PUNCH

EYELETS

EYELET SETTER

PENCIL

RULER

IRON

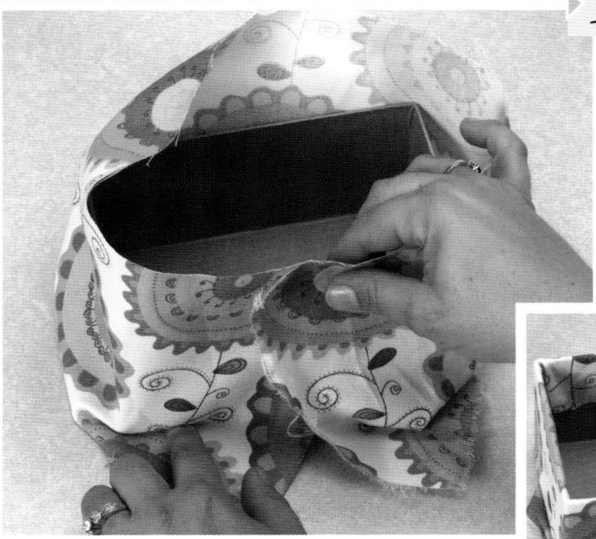

1 CUT FABRIC

Cut a length of fabric to fit around the sides of a
papier-mâché box, allowing about 2" (5cm) of fabric
around the top edge of the box and 1" (3cm) of fabric
(or less) around the bottom edge of the box .

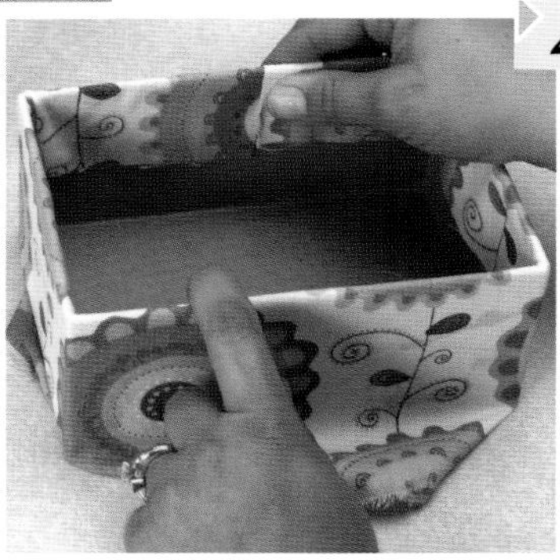

2 ADHERE FABRIC TO BOX

Use fabric glue to adhere the fabric
to the box. Fold the 2" (5cm) of extra
fabric into the box, adhering it to
the interior sides with glue.

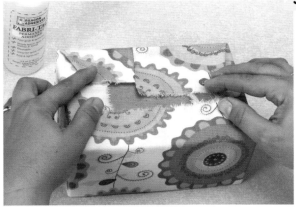

▶ *3* GLUE BOTTOM EDGES OF FABRIC

Fold the remaining fabric over the bottom edges of the box and glue the fabric to the bottom surface.

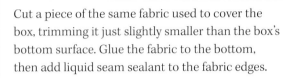

4 COVER BOTTOM SURFACE WITH FABRIC

Cut a piece of the same fabric used to cover the box, trimming it just slightly smaller than the box's bottom surface. Glue the fabric to the bottom, then add liquid seam sealant to the fabric edges.

▶ *5* LINE BOX INTERIOR

On a piece of cardstock, trace around the bottom edges of the box. Then, measure the sides of the box; using these dimensions, measure and mark pieces of the same cardstock to line the box interior. Cut out the bottom and side pieces. Use the cardstock to line the box, adhering the pieces to the bottom and side panels with fabric glue.

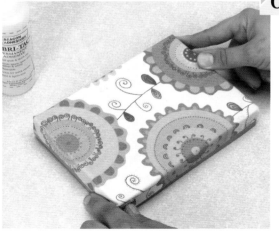

▶ *6* COVER BOX LID

Cut a piece of fabric 1" (3cm) wider and 1" (3cm) longer than the box top. Glue the fabric onto the top surface of the lid, centering the lid so there is ½" (12mm) of fabric on either side. Cut the corners of the fabric at an angle, then glue the corners in place for a mitred look.

7 PREPARE FABRIC FOR SIDES OF LID

Measure the width of the box lid sides. Cut a long strip of fabric that is double this width. Fold in both sides of the strip to make the width equal to the sides of the box lid, then glue and iron the strip.

8 COVER SIDES OF LID

Glue the fabric strip around the sides of the lid. If the strip is not long enough to cover all four sides, repeat step 7 to make another strip. Line the lid of the box, as you did the bottom in step 5.

9 SET EYELETS

Determine a center placement for the eyelets on two opposing sides of the box. Punch one hole on each side, then set the eyelets with an eyelet setter.

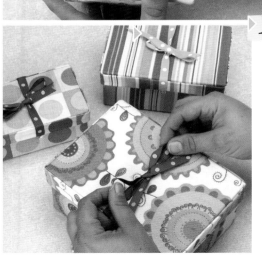

10 TIE BOW

Cut and place a length of ribbon around the exterior of the box, running each end through an eyelet. Put the lid on the box, then bring the ends of the ribbon on top of the lid and tie the ribbon in a bow. If desired, cover two more boxes with coordinating fabric to make a complete set.

Treasure Tins

IF YOU'RE LIKE ME, YOU RELISH THE OPPORTUNITY to create "trash-to-treasure" projects. There's just something gratifying about recycling an object, using your creativity to give it new life. One of my favorite recyclables is the Altoids mint tin, the kind that you might buy when standing in line at the supermarket. When the mints are gone, the real fun begins! I like to dress up the tins, covering them with paper and embellishing them with all kinds of sewing notions. The result is a little treasure tin to hold special mementos and trinkets. What a nice surprise this would make for a special friend!

MATERIALS AND TOOLS

METAL TIN
(SUCH AS AN ALTOIDS MINT TIN)

CARDSTOCK

DECORATIVE PAPER

RICE PAPER

FABRIC

FOAMCORE BOARD

SIX-STRAND EMBROIDERY FLOSS

EMBROIDERY NEEDLE

T-PIN

SCISSORS

PAPER GLUE

SPRAY PRIMER

SPRAY VARNISH

NO. 8 AND NO. 10 SHADER BRUSHES

ACRYLIC PAINT (METALLIC COLOR)

PIGMENT POWDER
(METALLIC TO MATCH ACRYLIC PAINT)

LIQUID EMBOSSING INK

DECORATIVE METAL LETTERS

1/2" (12MM) BUTTON COVERS
AND BUTTON COVER KIT

SANDPAPER

CLIP ART FRAME

SEWING MACHINE AND THREAD

PHOTOCOPIER

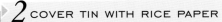

SAND AND PRIME TIN

With sandpaper, rough up the entire exterior surface of a mint tin. Continue sanding until you've removed all the painted lettering. When finished, spray the sanded box with primer in a well-ventilated area.

2 COVER TIN WITH RICE PAPER

Crumple a sheet of rice paper, then smooth it out. Cut two pieces of the rice paper, one to cover the top surface of the tin and one to cover the bottom. Glue the paper to the tin, then allow the glue to dry.

3 PAINT TIN

Using a no. 10 shader brush, paint the entire exterior surface of the tin with metallic acrylic paint.

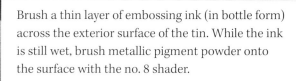

4 APPLY INK AND PIGMENT POWDER TO TIN

Brush a thin layer of embossing ink (in bottle form) across the exterior surface of the tin. While the ink is still wet, brush metallic pigment powder onto the surface with the no. 8 shader.

5 MAKE EMBROIDERED TAG

Photocopy a clipart frame onto a piece of cardstock, and trim the frame along its perimeter. Place the cardstock on a piece of foamcore board, then use a T-pin to poke evenly spaced holes along the frame design. (For this design, I poked holes along the oval of the frame.) Embroider the design with three strands of embroidery floss and an embroidery needle using a backstitch (see Making a Backstitch, page 14).

6 ATTACH FRAME

Glue the embroidered frame to the top of the tin, adding other embellishments as desired. Here I spelled out the word *Love* with decorative metal letters.

7 PREPARE PAPER TO LINE SIDES

Cut a narrow strip of paper to fit around the sides of the tin.
Using a sewing machine, make a zig-zag stitch along the center
of the strip.

8 GLUE STRIP TO SIDES

Glue the stitched paper strip
around the sides of the tin.

9 ADD BUTTON TO LID

Cut a piece of fabric a little wider than the button to be used
for the lid. Using a button kit, cover the button with the fabric.
When finished, glue the button to the front center of the tin.
Seal the tin by spraying it with varnish in a well-ventilated area.

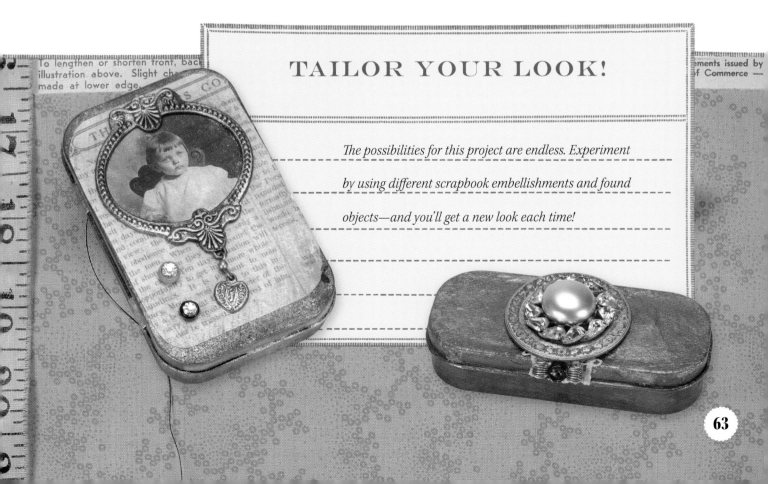

TAILOR YOUR LOOK!

The possibilities for this project are endless. Experiment

by using different scrapbook embellishments and found

objects—and you'll get a new look each time!

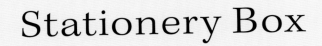

Stationery Box

THIS PROJECT IS AN EXCITING COMBINATION OF SURFACES and embellishments, which come together as a beautiful box to hold your stationery and correspondence. Fabric paper covers the exterior, fabric-covered foamcore pads line the interior, and ribbon and buttons add a decorative flair. After you've completed the box, use the leftover fabric and paper scraps to create a coordinating set of handmade stationery and cards. If you are making this project as a gift, beware—you may be tempted to keep it for yourself!

MATERIALS AND TOOLS

10¾" x 7¼" (27CM X 18CM) WOODEN BOX

DECORATIVE FABRIC PAPER

FABRIC

FOAMCORE BOARD

CHIPBOARD

BUTTON THREAD

26" (66CM) LENGTH OF ½" (12MM) DECORATIVE RIBBON

3" (8CM) LENGTH OF ⅛" (3MM) ROUND ELASTIC CORD

NEEDLE

SCISSORS

ROTARY CUTTER WITH PINKING BLADE

FABRIC GLUE

INDUSTRIAL-STRENGTH GLUE

LAMINATING LIQUID

ACRYLIC PAINT: GREEN

¾" (19MM) WASH BRUSH

MOTHER-OF-PEARL BUTTON

1" (3CM) ANTIQUE BUTTON WITH SHANK

MINIATURE DECORATIVE METAL FRAME (OPTIONAL)

DECORATIVE GLASS KNOB (FOR BOX HANDLE)

PENCIL

METAL RULER

HAND DRILL

SCREWDRIVER

BRAYER

HOT KNIFE TOOL

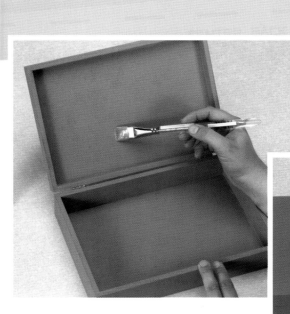

1 PAINT BOX

Paint the entire box, inside and out, with green acrylic paint, using a ¾" (19mm) wash brush. Let the paint dry completely.

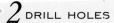

2 DRILL HOLES

Prepare for the clasp by hand-drilling two holes on the front center of the box—one hole on the base to accommodate the button and one hole on the lid to accommodate the elastic clasp loop. Use a ruler to determine the center point of the box lid's top surface. Mark the point, then drill a third hole through it.

▶ 3 COVER EXTERIOR

Measure the top and side surfaces of the box exterior. Following these measurements, use a rotary cutter to cut decorative fabric paper to cover each side of the exterior, cutting separate pieces for each side of the box lid and bottom. Use laminating liquid to adhere the paper to the box, then run a brayer over the paper to burnish it in place.

▶ 4 INSERT LID HANDLE

Locate the drilled hole on the box lid top, then puncture through the fabric paper to expose the hole. Insert a decorative knob into the hole and tighten to secure it in place, using a screwdriver, as necessary. If desired, embellish the lid by adding a miniature decorative frame around the knob, adhering it with industrial-strength glue.

▶ 5 CREATE LID INTERIOR

Using a hot knife, cut a sheet of foamcore to fit inside the interior of the lid. Cut a piece of fabric large enough to cover one side of the foamcore board. Adhere the fabric to the foamcore with fabric glue, pulling the ends of the fabric tightly over the edges of the foamcore before gluing in place.

▶ 6 LINE LID INTERIOR

Add two lengths of ribbon across the fabric-covered foamcore, forming an *X*, and adhere with glue. Pull the ends of the ribbon over each corner and secure with glue. Sew a button in the center of the *X*. Glue the fabric-covered foamcore into the lid interior.

7 LINE BOX BASE INTERIOR

Cut a piece of chipboard to fit into the interior base bottom, then cut a piece of fabric large enough to cover one side of the chipboard. Adhere the fabric to the chipboard with fabric glue, pulling the ends of the fabric tightly over the edges of the board before gluing in place.

8 LINE INTERIOR SIDES

Measure four panels of chipboard to fit along each interior side of the base. Cut four pieces of fabric to cover each panel, then adhere the fabric to the board with fabric glue. Adhere the fabric-covered panels to the interior sides, using fabric glue to secure.

9 ADD CLASP

Cut a length of elastic, then run both ends through the drilled hole on the box lid, forming a loop on the exterior of the lid. Be sure that the loop is large enough to fit around the button you'll be using for the clasp. Tie the two ends of the elastic together to secure the loop. Add industrial-strength glue to the back of the button. Insert the shank of the button into the drilled hole on the box base and through the liner added in step 8. Leave enough of the shank exposed to accommodate the elastic loop.

10 MAKE COORDINATING STATIONERY

Use scraps of the fabric paper to create coordinating notecards. Add embellishments, such as clay buttons and decorative borders, as desired. When finished, store the stationery in the box.

BOOKS AND JOURNALS

Never judge a book by its cover... unless its cover is made of beautiful fabric and embellished with lovely sewing notions! I enjoy coming up with new ways to incorporate sewing into book projects. Sometimes I start with a store-bought journal, and other times I construct the book myself. Either way, I'm always amazed by the possibilities that present themselves after a little brainstorming and exploration.

There is something very special about making books and journals as gifts for friends and family. Books are the perfect crafting combination of paper and fabric, and they offer the ideal opportunity to exercise some sewing creativity. When you give a handmade book as a gift, you get to pass that creative energy along to the recipient. Who knows—your inspiration may be contagious, and he or she may soon be filling the pages with his or her own crafty thoughts and artistic ideas. What better gift to give than a shot of creativity?

Back Pocket Booklet

WHO DOESN'T HAVE AN OLD PAIR OF JEANS in a closet, perhaps hopelessly outdated or two sizes too big? Don't pitch them— stitch them—because denim pockets are all you need to make this cute and clever booklet. The pockets serve as front and back covers, which can be embellished as desired. Denim jeans have a laid-back, comfortable feel, so I gave the pockets a fun and casual style, using colorful vintage fabric, ric-rac and a simple monogram. When finished, the covers not only protect the pages, they hold notes, cards and other paper mementos.

MATERIALS AND TOOLS

PAIR OF DENIM JEANS WITH TWO BACK POCKETS

TWO OR MORE 12" x 12" (30CM x 30CM)
SHEETS CARDSTOCK (DIFFERENT COLORS)

PRINTED FABRIC (FOR INSIDE COVER)

PRINTED FABRIC (FOR SPINE)

SMALL FABRIC SWATCHES (FOR THE FRONT COVER)

DECORATIVE RIBBON, 1/4" (6MM) WIDE
(FOR INTERIOR AND FOR EMBELLISHING NOTECARD)

RIC-RAC (FOR THE FRONT COVER)

SCISSORS

ROTARY CUTTER WITH PINKING BLADE

DOUBLE-SIDED FUSIBLE WEB
(STEAM-A-SEAM 2)

FABRIC GLUE

PAPER

PENCIL

ADHESIVE FELT LETTER
(FOR THE FRONT COVER)

IRON

SEWING MACHINE AND THREAD

1 CUT OUT DENIM POCKETS

Cut out both back pockets from a pair of denim jeans; remove the entire pockets, front and back, so that you can still slip things into the top openings.

2 CREATE AND ATTACH FABRIC SPINE

Cut two pieces of printed fabric, each 4" (10cm) wide and as long as the pockets. Using fabric glue, adhere the fabric pieces to one another, with the wrong sides facing each other. Place the two pockets face down on your work surface, side by side, so that the left edge of one is flush with the right edge of the other. Using fabric glue, adhere the fabric along the spine between the two pockets, as shown.

71

▶ 3 PLACE RIBBON INSIDE BOOK

Cut a 32" (81cm) length of ¼" (6mm) wide ribbon. With the pocket booklet open, use fabric glue to adhere the ribbon to the inside of the booklet, placing it in the center, as shown. If the ribbon has a right side, it should be face down.

▶ 4 CREATE INTERIOR LINING

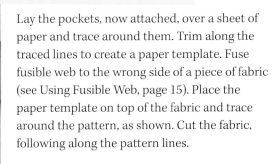

Lay the pockets, now attached, over a sheet of paper and trace around them. Trim along the traced lines to create a paper template. Fuse fusible web to the wrong side of a piece of fabric (see Using Fusible Web, page 15). Place the paper template on top of the fabric and trace around the pattern, as shown. Cut the fabric, following along the pattern lines.

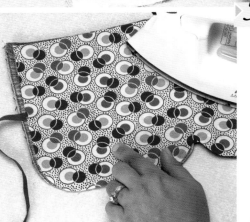

▶ 5 LINE INTERIOR

Remove the carrier sheet from the fabric cut in step 4. With the pocket booklet still open, place the fabric inside the booklet, directly over the ribbon. Fuse the fabric to the denim, using an iron.

▶ 6 CUT AND STITCH PAGES

Fold as many sheets of cardstock as desired to fit inside the booklet. Machine stitch along the center fold to make a booklet.

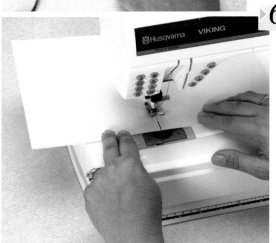

7 SECURE PAGES INSIDE BOOK

Adhere the stitched cardstock to the center of the booklet with fabric glue. Using a rotary cutter with a pinking blade, cut a ¼" (6mm)-wide strip the same length as the stitched cardstock's spine and fuse fusible webbing to the wrong side of the fabric. Open the booklet, then iron the strip over the center stitching.

8 EMBELLISH FRONT COVER

Choose and prepare embellishments for the cover. Apply the embellishments, such as fabric swatches, felt letters, ric-rac and buttons, to the front cover with fabric glue.

9 MAKE NOTECARD FOR FRONT POCKET

Cut a sheet of cardstock to put inside the pocket of the front cover. Embellish the notecard as desired, then slip it into the pocket. Tie the ribbon in a bow to keep the booklet closed.

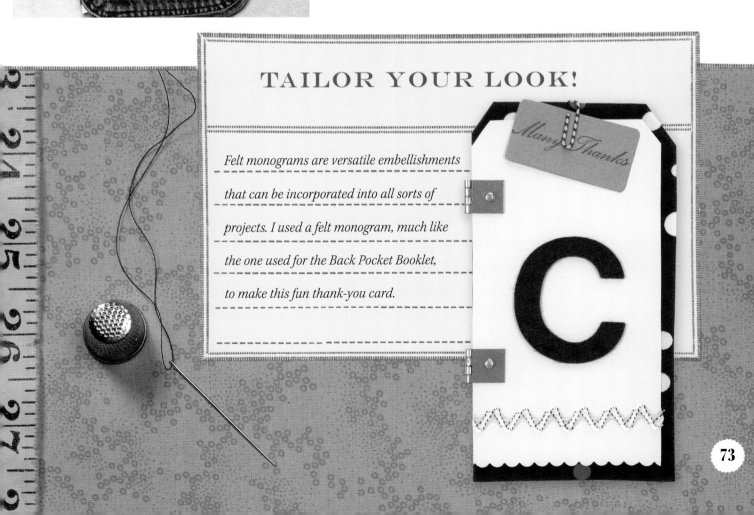

TAILOR YOUR LOOK!

Felt monograms are versatile embellishments that can be incorporated into all sorts of projects. I used a felt monogram, much like the one used for the Back Pocket Booklet, to make this fun thank-you card.

Many Thanks

73

No Stitchin' Kitchen Book

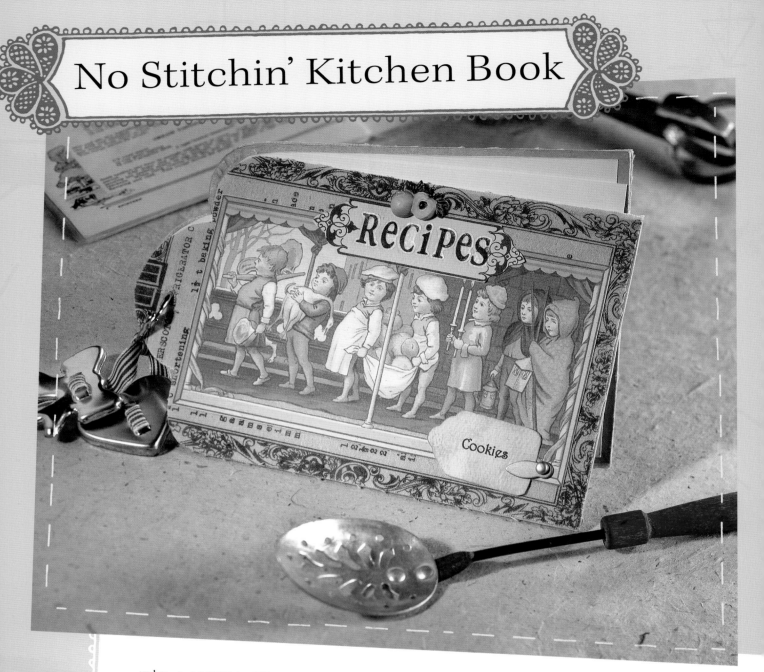

IT'S A THRILL TO PASS DOWN OLD FAMILY RECIPES from
generation to generation. This project offers a fantastic way to keep all
your favorite recipes organized and in one place in the kitchen. And,
it's super easy, using fabric and ribbon, with no stitching required!
Why not give this book as a special family gift? Ask your family members
to provide you with their favorite recipes, then compile them and create
multiple copies of the book. Such a unique and personalized gift is sure
to be treasured *and* used for years to come.

MATERIALS AND TOOLS

TWO 7" (18CM) PAPIER-MÂCHÉ TAGS

TEA-DYED MUSLIN

TEXT-WEIGHT PAPER AND/OR
OLD FAMILY RECIPE PAGES

CARDSTOCK

RIBBON

SCISSORS

PINKING SHEARS (OPTIONAL)

HOLE PUNCH

DOUBLE-SIDED FUSIBLE WEB
(STEAM-A-SEAM 2)

FABRIC GLUE

MINIATURE COOKIE CUTTERS

BINDER RING (SUCH AS A KEY CHAIN RING)

LETTER STICKERS (OPTIONAL)

RESIN EMBELLISHMENTS (OPTIONAL)

PENCIL

IRON

PHOTOCOPIER

1 APPLY FUSIBLE WEB TO MUSLIN

Cut a piece of tea-dyed muslin larger than 8½" x 11"
(22cm x 28cm) (see Creating a Tea-Dyed Surface, page
77). Cut an 8½" x 11" (22cm x 28cm) sheet of fusible web.
Fuse the fusible web to the muslin (see Using Fusible
Web, page 15), then trim the excess fabric so that you are
left with an 8½" x 11" (22cm x 28cm) sheet.

2 COPY RECIPE PAGES ONTO MUSLIN

Photocopy original recipe pages onto the fabric side
of the muslin sheet. This is easily done by running the
muslin sheet through the photocopier; just make sure
that the muslin is face down in the paper well of the
photo copier.

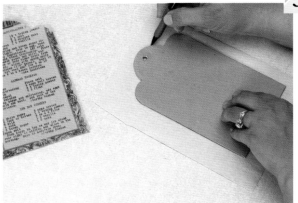

▶3 TRACE AND CUT OUT TAGS

Trace a papier-mâché tag twice onto the photocopied muslin, then cut the two tags out. For an extra decorative touch, you can trim the edges with pinking shears.

▶4 FUSE MUSLIN TO TAGS

Peel off the carrier sheet from the muslin tags to expose the sticky surface, then adhere the muslin tags to the papier-mâché tags. Iron the tags to adhere the two surfaces together.

▶5 ADD DECORATIVE IMAGE TO COVER

Select a decorative image to use for the front cover tag, then print or copy the image onto cardstock. (I used a Vintage Workshop CD-ROM and printed an image from my computer.) Cut the image out, then glue it onto one of the tags.

▶6 EMBELLISH COVER

Add decorative embellishments to the cover as desired. For this book, I decorated the cover with a *Cookies* tag, a *Recipes* tag and a stick-on fruit embellishment.

7 MAKE RECIPE PAGES

Trace a papier-mâché tag onto several sheets of white or cream text-weight paper for recipe pages. Cut out the tag shapes, then stack them. Place the stack between the book covers. Use a hole punch to punch through all the pages so that they can be assembled in step 9.

8 PREPARE RING

Place a few miniature cookie cutters on a length of ribbon, then tie the ribbon onto a binder ring.

9 ASSEMBLE BOOK

Open the ring, slide one end through the punched holes of the pages, then close the ring to secure.

SPRAY THE FABRIC OR PAPER WITH GLOSSY SAFFRON OR WOOD-TONE ACRYLIC SPRAY.

Creating a Tea-Dyed Surface

Several projects call for "tea-dyed" paper or fabric. This gives the material a warm, antiqued look. This is a good technique to know for all kinds of craft projects. You can actually dye with tea, but here are four other options to achieve the same look.

DYE THE PAPER OR FABRIC WITH COMMERCIAL DYE, SUCH AS TAN RIT. LARGE PIECES OF FABRIC CAN BE DYED IN A WASHING MACHINE WITH COMMERCIAL DYE ADDED, OR SMALL PIECES CAN BE DYED IN A BASIN WITH A MIXTURE OF DYE AND HOT WATER, AS SHOWN. FOR A MOTTLED OR UNEVEN EFFECT, FILL A SPRAY BOTTLE WITH THE MIXED DYE AND SPRITZ IT ON AS DESIRED.

APPLY BROWN OR TEA-COLOR INK ONTO THE PAPER OR FABRIC.

MAKE TEA WITH SEVERAL TEA BAGS OR COFFEE WITH INSTANT COFFEE CRYSTALS AND SPRAY OR IMMERSE THE PAPER OR FABRIC IN THE SOLUTION. YOU CAN ALSO EXPERIMENT WITH HERBAL TEAS, SUCH AS BLUEBERRY, FOR SUBTLE TINTS, OR GENTLY RUB THE TEA BAG ONTO THE PAPER OR FABRIC SURFACE TO GET A SPOTTED LOOK.

Barkcloth-Is-Back Book

BARKCLOTH, A HEAVY COTTON-WEAVE FABRIC, is often
associated with the vintage look of the 1950s. Along with its distinctive
nubby texture, the fabric is famous for its bold prints and funky patterns.
In its heyday, barkcloth was a fashionable choice for furniture upholstery
and window coverings. These days, barkcloth is enjoying a resurgence
in popularity, as more people rediscover its hip allure. As a barkcloth
addict, I love finding ways to incorporate the fabric into projects. Here,
I cover a store-bought journal with vintage barkcloth, transforming a
boring book to a classic look.

MATERIALS AND TOOLS

JOURNAL

BARKCLOTH

CARDSTOCK

COORDINATING PRINTED FABRIC AND FABRIC PAPERS

MANILA FILE FOLDER

SCISSORS

PINKING SHEARS

DOUBLE-SIDED FUSIBLE WEB (STEAM-A-SEAM 2)

FABRIC GLUE

SPRAY ADHESIVE

INDUSTRIAL-STRENGTH GLUE

BLACK ACRYLIC PAINT (OPTIONAL)

PAINTBRUSH

DECORATIVE RUBBER STAMP

CLEAR EMBOSSING INK PAD

PINK-GOLD PIGMENT POWDER

AIR-DRY CLAY

MINIATURE DECORATIVE METAL FRAME

DISAPPEARING MARKER

IRON

SEWING MACHINE AND THREAD

PASTA MACHINE

CRAZY QUILT TEMPLATE OF YOUR CHOICE

PHOTOCOPIER

1 CREATE COVER FOR JOURNAL

Lay a piece of barkcloth on your work surface, right side down, then open the journal and lay it on top of the fabric. Use disappearing marker to trace the perimeter of the journal onto the fabric.
Use scissors to cut out the fabric cover, trimming about 1½" (4cm) beyond the traced lines. Place the cut fabric on your work surface, again right side down, and place the open journal on top.
Pull the fabric around the edges of the front and back covers to make sure it will fit correctly.

2 COVER JOURNAL

In a well-ventilated area, coat the surface of the journal cover with spray adhesive. Adhere the cut fabric to the journal, then use your hands to burnish the fabric to the surface.

3 WORK FABRIC OVER EDGES

Make the fabric cover taut by working the excess fabric around the journal's edges. Use fabric glue to glue down any stray pieces of fabric that may be sticking up.

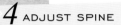

4 ADJUST SPINE

Work the fabric along the spine, tucking and gluing any excess fabric into the spine with one end of a pencil or scissors.

5 LINE COVER INTERIORS

Cut two pieces of cardstock, one to line the inside of the front cover and the other to line the back. Use fabric glue to adhere the cardstock panels to the inside of each cover.

6 PREPARE QUILT PATTERN

Photocopy a crazy quilt pattern of your choice. (You can find patterns in books, in stores and even online.) Use spray adhesive to glue the photocopied pattern onto a manila file folder (or other stiff paper) for support, then cut the pattern apart into individual pieces.

7 CHOOSE AND PREPARE FABRIC

Choose several different fabrics and fabric papers for your quilt block, selecting colors and patterns that coordinate. Fuse fusible web (see Using Fusible Web, page 15) to the wrong side of the fabric and paper, then trim any excess fusible web as necessary.

8 TRACE PATTERN PIECES ONTO FABRIC

Place the pattern pieces face down on the fusible-web side of the fabric and fabric paper. Trace the perimeter of each pattern piece onto the fabric and paper, then cut out each piece.

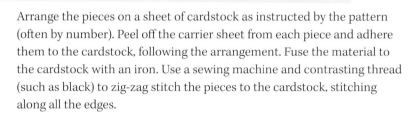

9 ASSEMBLE AND ADHERE PIECES TO CARDSTOCK

Arrange the pieces on a sheet of cardstock as instructed by the pattern (often by number). Peel off the carrier sheet from each piece and adhere them to the cardstock, following the arrangement. Fuse the material to the cardstock with an iron. Use a sewing machine and contrasting thread (such as black) to zig-zag stitch the pieces to the cardstock, stitching along all the edges.

10 TRACE HEART ONTO PATTERN

Once your crazy quilt pattern is assembled and glued in place, draw or trace a heart onto the pattern surface.

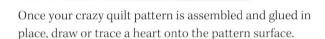

▶ *11* CUT OUT HEART

Use pinking shears to cut out the heart shape.

▶ *12* MOUNT HEART ONTO FABRIC

Use fabric glue to adhere the heart to a coordinating piece of fabric. Trim around the heart with pinking shears, leaving a ¼" (6mm) border around the edges.

NOTE: *The coordinating fabric piece can first be backed or fused to paper for added support.*

▶ *13* ADHERE HEART TO COVER

Use fabric glue to adhere the heart to the cover, placing as desired.

▶ *14* PREPARE CLAY FOR BUTTON

Run a piece of air-dry clay through the pasta machine on its thinnest setting.

**JUST SEW
YOU KNOW:**
WHAT IS IT?

Air-dry clay comes in plastic packs and is available at craft stores. It's not messy and is great for creating buttons and embellishments.

15 STAMP CLAY

Press a decorative rubber stamp into a clear embossing ink pad, then stamp the clay with the inked rubber stamp.

16 CURE AND PAINT BUTTON

Cut the button design out of the clay. Set aside and let dry. When dry, paint the button surface as desired with acrylic paint. Allow the paint to dry completely.

17 APPLY PIGMENT POWDER TO BUTTON AND FRAME

Press the button into the clear embossing ink pad. While the ink is still wet, dust pigment powder across the surface with a brush. Do the same with the miniature decorative frame, pressing the front of the frame into the clear ink pad and immediately dusting with pigment powder.

18 ADD BUTTON AND FRAME

Using industrial-strength glue, adhere the frame and the clay button to the heart.

TAILOR YOUR LOOK!

Keep your paperwork organized in this nifty file holder. Just cover a simple accordion-file portfolio with your favorite barkcloth, then add a fabric-covered button to match. This particular pattern showcases the vintage 1950s look for which barkcloth is so well known.

83

Recycled Pattern Book

IF YOU'VE BEEN SEWING YOUR WHOLE LIFE, you might have a stack of old, tattered garment patterns, stored away somewhere. Why not recycle those patterns? With this project, you can use a pattern to cover a gift booklet. Old patterns are especially interesting, and they create a vintage look, whether you photocopy the pattern onto tissue paper or use the real thing. If you don't have a bunch of patterns readily available, don't worry—used patterns are easy to find at flea markets or garage sales (and new patterns are always available at fabric stores). Try baby patterns for a baby booklet or a wedding gown pattern for a bridal album.

MATERIALS AND TOOLS

SMALL PRE-MADE BOOKLET, WITH RIBBON

12" x 12" (30CM x 30CM) SHEETS DECORATIVE
CARDSTOCK IN COORDINATING PATTERNS

OLD GARMENT PATTERN OR TAN TISSUE PAPER

TEA-DYED, NEEDLED COTTON BATTING

NEEDLE AND THREAD

PINKING SHEARS

DOUBLE-SIDED FUSIBLE WEB (STEAM-A-SEAM 2)

PAPER GLUE

BUTTONS

PENCIL

IRON

PHOTOCOPIER

▶ 1 TRACE COVER

Place a sheet of decorative paper wrong side up on
your work surface. Open the booklet and place it on
the paper, then trace around the booklet.

▶ 2 ATTACH COVER

Cut out the cover, trimming
along the traced lines with pinking shears. Glue the decorative
paper to the book cover with
paper glue.

▶ 3 PREPARE TISSUE PAPER

Fuse fusible web to an old garment pattern or a crumpled sheet of tan tissue paper (see Just Sew You Know, page 87). If you use tissue paper, copy and print a pattern onto the paper once it has been backed with fusible web (see Using Fusible Web, page 15).

▶ 4 FUSE BATTING TO PAPER

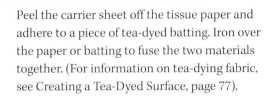

Peel the carrier sheet off the tissue paper and adhere to a piece of tea-dyed batting. Iron over the paper or batting to fuse the two materials together. (For information on tea-dying fabric, see Creating a Tea-Dyed Surface, page 77).

▶ 5 ADD PATTERN TO COVER

Trim the batting with pinking shears. Adhere the batting-backed pattern to the front cover with fabric glue.

▶ 6 MAKE "IDEAS" TAG

Fuse a small piece of decorative paper to a small piece of batting for a front tag. Once fused, cut the batting-backed paper into a tag shape. Print an *Ideas* label, mount it to a slightly larger piece of decorative paper, then trim and glue the mounted label to the tag.

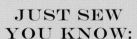

7 SEW BUTTON ON TAG

Sew two buttons onto the tag, one on either side of the *Ideas* label.

8 GLUE TAG TO COVER

Place the tag as desired on the front cover and adhere with glue.

JUST SEW YOU KNOW:
CREATING READY-TO-USE FAUX VINTAGE PAPER

An old garment pattern offers a special vintage look. Do you have an old pattern, but you don't want to cut it up? No problem. Crumple a sheet of tan tissue paper, then smooth it out on your work surface. Cut an 8½" x 11" (22cm x 28cm) sheet of fusible web, and cut the tissue paper a little larger than 8½" x 11" (22cm x 28cm). Smooth the tissue paper onto the fusible web, then fuse with an iron. Trim any excess tissue paper along the edges. You now have a sheet of paper that can be run through the photocopier.

TAILOR YOUR LOOK!

For this book, I stayed with the red and yellow gingham theme but incorporated a heart motif. You are the artist, so go with your own style! Design your own version, using ribbon, buttons and other scrapbook embellishments.

Gardener's Journal

KNOW A GARDENING ENTHUSIAST? THIS DIARY WILL BE one gift they'll really "dig"! Surprise a green-thumbed friend with an inspirational garden journal. This project isn't just pretty—it is also practical for use in the garden. A coat of varnish seals the front cover, rendering the book a resilient outdoor garden accessory. So, between digging, planting and watering, busy gardeners can jot down all their horticultural notes in one place. Notes can also be stashed in the cover pocket, which is constructed in the shape of an old-fashioned fan.

MATERIALS AND TOOLS

COMPOSITION BOOK

12" x 12" (30CM x 30CM) SHEETS OF DECORATIVE CARDSTOCK AND FABRIC PAPER (COORDINATING PATTERNS)

EMBROIDERY FLOSS

RIBBON

LACE TRIM

EMBROIDERY NEEDLE

T-PIN

SCISSORS

SCALLOP SHEARS

LAMINATING LIQUID

BASTING GLUE

PAPER GLUE

INDUSTRIAL-STRENGTH GLUE

HOT GLUE GUN

GLOSS VARNISH

ANTIQUING VARNISH

SPRAY GLOSS VARNISH

TINTED WALNUT INK

OIL PAINT STICK

1 ½" (4CM) WASH BRUSH

1" (3CM) STENCIL BRUSH

JOURNAL RUBBER STAMP

ALPHABET RUBBER STAMPS (TO SPELL *GARDEN*)

MANILA TAGS

PAPER FLOWERS

PEARL BEADS (WITH HOLES)

DESIGN STENCIL OF YOUR CHOICE

PENCIL

BRAYER

RULER

SEWING MACHINE AND THREAD

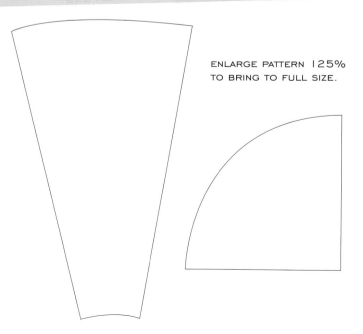

ENLARGE PATTERN 125% TO BRING TO FULL SIZE.

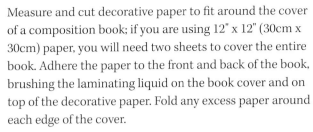

1 COVER BOOK

Measure and cut decorative paper to fit around the cover of a composition book; if you are using 12" x 12" (30cm x 30cm) paper, you will need two sheets to cover the entire book. Adhere the paper to the front and back of the book, brushing the laminating liquid on the book cover and on top of the decorative paper. Fold any excess paper around each edge of the cover.

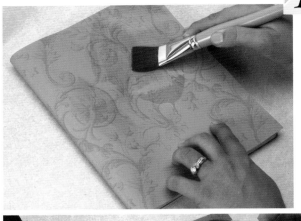

2 BURNISH AND VARNISH COVER

Use a brayer to eliminate air bubbles and burnish the paper in place. After the laminating liquid has dried completely, use a 1½" (4cm) wash brush to apply gloss varnish to the front and back of the book.

3 APPLY TOP STRIP AND COAT WITH VARNISH

Cut a 2" (5cm)-wide strip of decorative paper, then adhere it along the top edge of the book with laminating liquid. Allow the liquid to dry completely, then coat the cover with gloss varnish. When the gloss varnish has dried, add a coat of antiquing varnish.

4 CREATE FAN PIECES

Trace four fan pieces onto decorative cardstock or fabric paper using the template provided. Cut out each fan piece.

5 ARRANGE AND GLUE FAN PIECES

Place the four pieces in a fan arrangement on a piece of cardstock, as shown. Adhere the pieces in place with basting glue.

6 STITCH PIECES IN PLACE

Using a sewing machine, zig-zag stitch along each edge of the four pieces. Then, zig-zag stitch along the edge of the fan's outer curve. Cut two wedge shapes of cardstock or fabric paper to fit in the lower center of the fan, cutting the rounded edge with scallop shears, then glue in place. Use scallop shears to cut along the rounded edge of the fan, as shown.

7 APPLY VARNISH

Apply a coat of antiquing varnish over the stitched fan. Allow the varnish to dry completely.

8 GLUE FAN TO COVER

Using industrial-strength glue, adhere the varnished fan to the bottom right corner of the front cover. Glue only along the bottom and right edge of the cover so that the fan can function as a pocket.

9 EMBELLISH COVER

Glue embellishments, such as lace trim, to the cover with paper glue. I also added a paper flower, which I colored subtly with a pink oil paint stick, then adhered with hot glue. Stamp the words of your choice on the cover; I stamped *Journal* below the decorative trim and *Garden* along the fan pocket.

▶ *10* DYE AND INK TAGS

Dye tags in a tea solution (see Creating a Tea-Dyed Surface, page 77). When the dye has dried, add a light layer of tinted walnut ink to give each tag a richer tone, as shown. Allow the ink to dry completely.

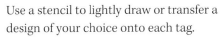

▶ *11* TRANSFER DESIGN ONTO TAG

Use a stencil to lightly draw or transfer a design of your choice onto each tag.

NOTE: *You can use a hot-iron transfer design for this step, if desired.*

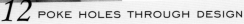

▶ *12* POKE HOLES THROUGH DESIGN

Use a T-pin to poke evenly spaced holes through the pencil lines.

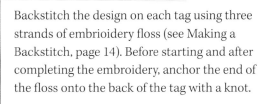

▶ *13* BACKSTITCH DESIGN

Backstitch the design on each tag using three strands of embroidery floss (see Making a Backstitch, page 14). Before starting and after completing the embroidery, anchor the end of the floss onto the back of the tag with a knot.

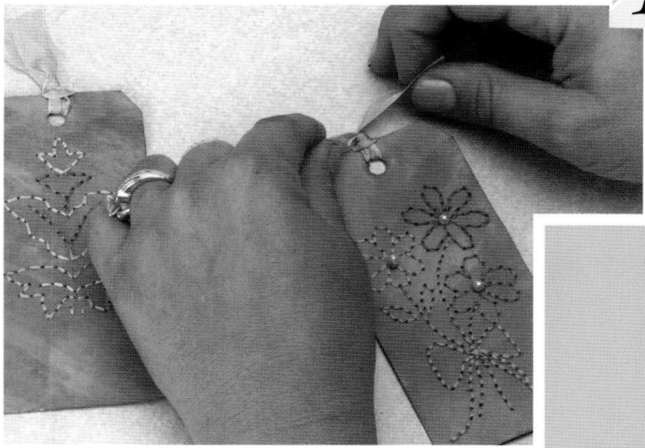

14 EMBELLISH TAGS

Tie a ribbon through each tag decoration. If desired, sew pearl beads onto the embroidered designs.

15 LINE INSIDE OF COVERS

Cut two sheets of cardstock, one to fit inside each cover. Glue one sheet inside the front cover and one sheet inside the back cover.

16 VARNISH BOOK EXTERIOR

Seal the book exterior by spraying a coat of gloss varnish over the front and back covers. Seal the tags as well.

17 INSERT TAGS

Slide the embroidered tags into the fan-shaped pocket, allowing the ribbon ends to stick out.

To lengthen or shorten front, back illustration above. Slight changes made at lower edge.

ments issued b
f Commerce —

TAILOR YOUR LOOK!

Try machine stitching cardstock

together to make a creative file folder.

I attached a paper-quilted fan

pocket, similar to the one used for

the Gardener's Journal, to spruce

up the exterior of this folder.

a perfect moment

FRAMES AND WALLHANGINGS

I'm constantly seeking new ways to make my home warm and welcoming while giving it a personal touch. Quite often, I've found that wallhangings are the easiest means of establishing both a comfortable atmosphere and personalized style. So in my house, there's always space on the walls for one more picture. Wallhangings are frequently the first things houseguests notice, drawing "oohs" and "ahhs." Given such praise, I am extra proud to tell my guests that the wall decorations are handmade—without revealing how simple these projects actually are to make!

In the previous sections, you've combined sewing and papercrafting techniques to create cards, boxes and books. In this last section, you'll use those techniques to take your projects to a new level—the walls of your home! These frames and wallhangings are as cute and clever as they are functional. And remember, the style of each project can easily be altered to match your own home décor.

Paper Patchwork Frame

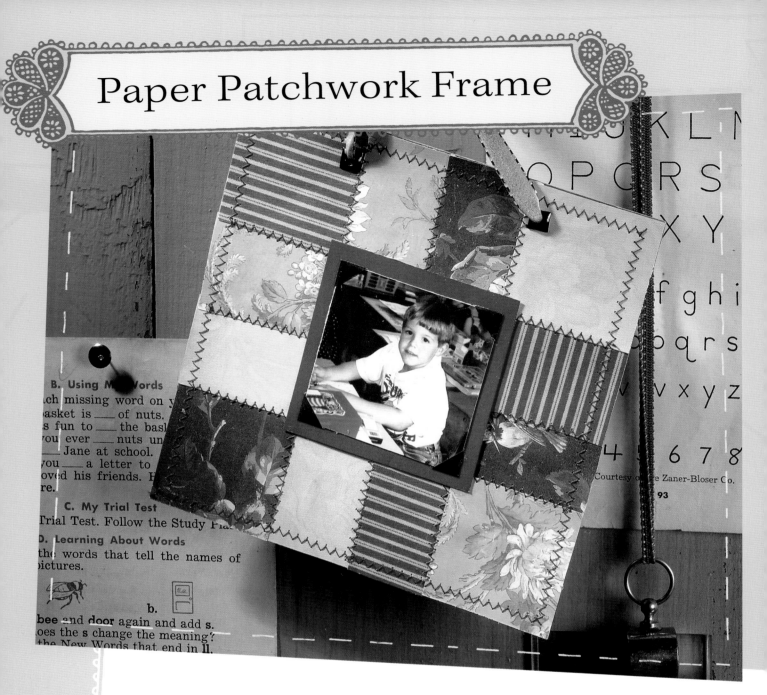

THIS LITTLE FRAME IS SO VERSATILE, you can make a version
of it for nearly every occasion—birthdays, weddings, anniversaries, baby
showers and more. Consider creating a series of these patchwork paper
frames to document the childhood of your son, daughter, niece or nephew.
Make a frame for every birthday, then have the child make a handprint on
the back. Display the frames at every birthday celebration, and you'll
have a "patchwork" of special memories.

MATERIALS AND TOOLS

PHOTOGRAPH TO FRAME

COORDINATING DECORATIVE PAPER
(FOUR SHEETS, EACH A DIFFERENT DESIGN)

SOLID-COLOR CARDSTOCK

CHIPBOARD

RIBBON

SCISSORS

ROTARY CUTTER WITH STRAIGHT BLADE

PAPER GLUE

BASTING GLUE

PHOTO CORNERS

EYELETS

EYELET SETTER

METAL RULER

SEWING MACHINE AND THREAD

1 CUT STRIPS OF DECORATIVE PAPER

Use a rotary cutter with a straight blade to cut four sheets of decorative paper into 2" (5cm) strips.

NOTE: *For easier cutting, simply stack the paper so that the edges are flush, then attach them with a staple in the upper left corner.*

2 ADHERE PAPER STRIPS TO CARDSTOCK

Cut a 6½" (16cm) square of colored cardstock. Cut a 2" (5cm) square from each paper strip, then adhere one piece to each corner of the cardstock with a dab of basting glue. Cut the remaining strips into random lengths. Use a dab of basting glue to adhere the random pieces along the sides of the cardstock. These pieces should form a "frame," leaving a blank center on the cardstock.

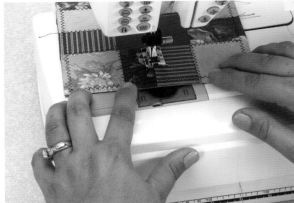

▶3 STITCH PAPER PIECES IN PLACE

Machine stitch the paper pieces in place, using a zig-zag stitch along the edges to join the pieces to one another and secure them to the cardstock.

▶4 MOUNT PHOTOGRAPH

Cut the photograph to a 2½" (6cm) square and a piece of colored cardstock to a 3" (8cm) square. Place photo corners on the photo, then mount it to the cardstock with paper glue.

▶5 MOUNT PHOTOGRAPH TO FRAME

Adhere the photograph to the center of the paper patchwork frame using paper glue.

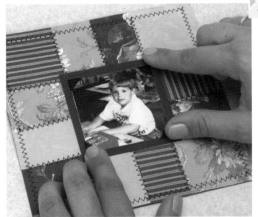

▶6 CUT CHIPBOARD

Cut a piece of chipboard to a 6½" (16cm) square.

7 MOUNT FRAME TO CHIPBOARD

Adhere the chipboard to the back of the patchwork frame with paper glue.

8 APPLY EYELETS TO FRAME

Use an eyelet setter to set two eyelets along the top panel of the frame, placing each ½" (12mm) from the top edge and 1¾" (4cm) in from the side edges.

9 ADD RIBBON HANGER

Run a length of decorative ribbon through the eyelets to create a hanger, then knot each end of the ribbon to secure it. Use the ribbon to hang the frame as desired.

JUST SEW YOU KNOW:
IT'S EASIER THAN IT SEAMS

When machine stitching, there are a few easy ways to stitch in a straight line. A good guide is the edge of the presser foot or the machine's guidelines, usually provided on the machine bed. You can also draw a straight guideline on fabric with a disappearing marker; stitch along the line while the ink is fresh, and then sit back and relax as the ink disappears!

Lid and Leftovers Frame

YOU'VE PROBABLY FACED THE COMMON CRAFTING dilemma of what to do with scraps and leftovers from previous projects. Tiny bits of paper, fabric, lace, ribbon and other embellishments litter your work space, and you just can't bring yourself to throw them away—sound familiar? If so, gather your scraps for this project, which is a unique frame made from a cigar box lid. Choose a favorite photograph to feature in the design, then let your scraps determine the style of your frame.

MATERIALS AND TOOLS

CIGAR BOX (WITH LID INTACT)

PHOTOGRAPH

FABRIC PAPER

DECORATIVE PAPER
(COORDINATING WITH THE FABRIC PAPER)

CHIPBOARD

EMBROIDERY FLOSS
(COORDINATING WITH THE PAPERS)

RIBBON

LACE, 1" (3CM) WIDE

BRAIDED TRIM, 1/4" (6MM) WIDE

EMBROIDERY NEEDLE

SCISSORS

PAPER GLUE

INDUSTRIAL-STRENGTH GLUE

CLEAR TAPE

LIQUID SEAM SEALANT (SUCH AS FRAY CHECK)

ROUND, METAL DECORATIVE SCRAPBOOK
EMBELLISHMENT, WITH HOLES AROUND
THE PERIMETER

MINIATURE DECORATIVE METAL FRAME

8MM PEARL BEADS (OPTIONAL)

18 KT. GOLD LEAF PEN

TWO SCREW EYES

AWL

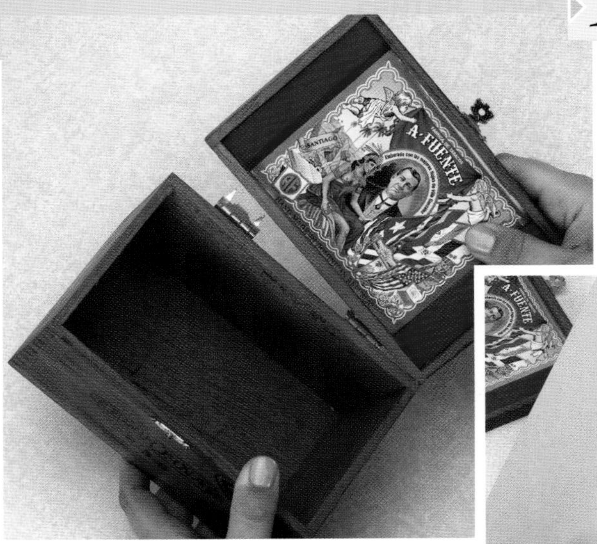

1 REMOVE BOX LID

Remove the box lid by pulling it off the
cigar box.

2 CUT CHIPBOARD

Cut a piece of chipboard to the
same dimensions as the interior
of the cigar box lid.

▶3 CUT AND ADHERE PAPER TO CHIPBOARD

Cut a sheet of decorative paper to the same dimensions as the chipboard. Use paper glue to adhere the paper to the chipboard.

▶4 FRAME PHOTOGRAPH

Place the miniature decorative metal frame over the photograph to determine how you want the image to be cropped. Add paper glue to the back of the frame, then place it over the photograph as desired. Once the glue has dried, trim the excess paper around the perimeter of the frame.

▶5 MAKE METAL EMBELLISHMENTS

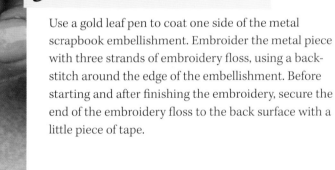

Use a gold leaf pen to coat one side of the metal scrapbook embellishment. Embroider the metal piece with three strands of embroidery floss, using a backstitch around the edge of the embellishment. Before starting and after finishing the embroidery, secure the end of the embroidery floss to the back surface with a little piece of tape.

▶6 CREATE DESIGN ON LID

Cut strips of lace, fabric paper and braided trim to fit across the top and bottom of the paper-covered chipboard, then glue them in place. Apply liquid seam sealant to the ends of the lace. Create and add more components, placing them and adhering them as desired (see Sew Easy Tip, page 103). Use industrial-strength glue to adhere heavier components.

7 ADHERE CHIPBOARD TO LID

Secure the embellished chipboard to the cigar box lid using industrial-strength glue.

8 ADD SCREW EYES

Determine the placement of the screw eyes on the frame, then use an awl or pointed object to make two small holes as desired. Insert one screw eye into each hole, then twist the screw eyes into the wood, securing them in place.

9 ADD RIBBON

Place a length of ribbon through the screw eyes, then tie the ribbon; this will allow you to hang the frame. When finished, add finishing touches—such as pearl beads—as desired.

SEW EASY TIP

I used a leaf pen to color the metal letters for this project. This is an easy way to customize ready-made embellishments.

TAILOR YOUR LOOK!

This wall-hanging was also made from a cigar box lid. I chose a vintage French postcard as the focal point of the design, then mixed and matched red and white embellishments for an eclectic look.

Clipboard Collage Frame

A SIMPLE CLIPBOARD SURFACE CAN ADD an interesting twist to any collage project. I chose an antique photograph as the centerpiece for this collage. Then, to complement the look of the aged photo, I infused the design with a classic, old-time style. Vintage floral patterns and ribbon set the tone, and an embroidery hoop and small hand-made "quilt-let" add the ultimate old-fashioned touch. Want a more modern look? Keep the clipboard, but use bolder colors and more contemporary patterns.

MATERIALS AND TOOLS

PHOTOGRAPH

9" (23CM) CLIPBOARD

DECORATIVE CARDSTOCK

DECORATIVE PAPER

DECORATIVE COTTON FABRIC

MUSLIN

BATTING

BUTTON THREAD

RIBBON

NEEDLE

SCISSORS

LAMINATING LIQUID

PAPER GLUE

ACRYLIC PAINT: IVORY, BLACK

¾" (19MM) WASH BRUSH

DECORATIVE BUTTONS

5" (13CM) OVAL EMBROIDERY HOOP

FINE-GRAIN SANDPAPER

BRAYER

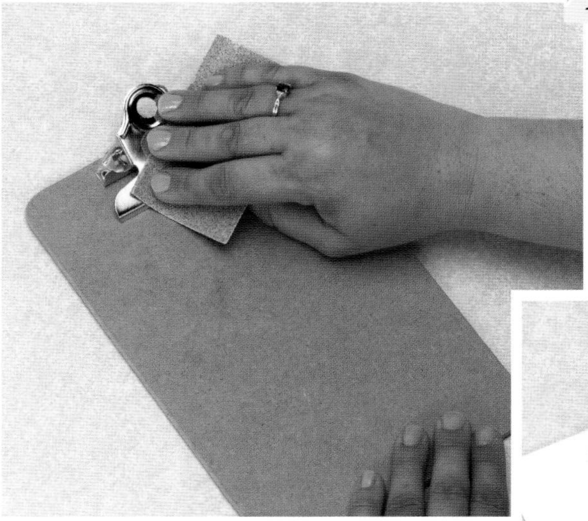

1 SAND CLIPBOARD

Gently sand the entire surface of the
clipboard, including the metal clip.

2 PAINT CLIPBOARD

Using a ¾" (19mm) wash brush, apply
one coat of ivory acrylic paint to the clipboard. Let the paint dry completely, then
add another coat. When finished, apply
one coat of black acrylic paint to the
metal clip. Let the paint dry completely,
then add another coat.

3 PAINT HOOP

Apply one coat of black acrylic paint to the embroidery hoop.

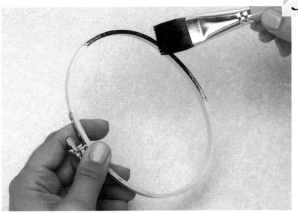

4 COVER CLIPBOARD WITH PAPER

Trim a sheet of decorative paper to the size of the clipboard, from below the clip to the bottom edge of the board. With a clean brush, adhere the paper to the clipboard using laminating liquid.

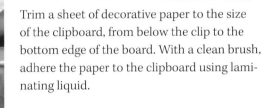

5 BURNISH PAPER TO BOARD

Burnish the decorative paper to the clipboard surface with a brayer.

6 SEAL PAPER

Brush a layer of laminating liquid (or decoupage medium) onto the clipboard surface and clip.

▶ 7 MOUNT PHOTOGRAPH

Trim your photograph to the desired size. Glue it to cardstock, then trim around it, leaving a thin border. Continue mounting onto cardstock and trimming until you have as many borders as you desire.

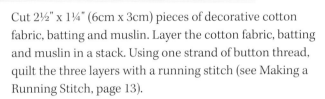
▶ 8 PREPARE FABRIC EMBELLISHMENT

Cut 2½" x 1¼" (6cm x 3cm) pieces of decorative cotton fabric, batting and muslin. Layer the cotton fabric, batting and muslin in a stack. Using one strand of button thread, quilt the three layers with a running stitch (see Making a Running Stitch, page 13).

▶ 9 BEGIN ADDING EMBELLISHMENTS

With paper glue, begin adhering embellishments to the clipboard, adding the photograph first, followed by the hoop to frame the image. Tie a ribbon around the clipboard, right under the clip, and tie it in a bow. Add a decorative button to the clip.

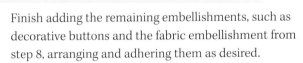
▶ 10 FINISH ADDING EMBELLISHMENTS

Finish adding the remaining embellishments, such as decorative buttons and the fabric embellishment from step 8, arranging and adhering them as desired.

Note Board To Be Noticed

WHAT ROOM COULDN'T USE A HANDY NOTE BOARD?

Make this board, and you've created an easy way to spruce up your kitchen, your office or even your kids' bedrooms—and keep your family organized at the same time! Available at your local home improvement store, homosote board is a sturdy, inexpensive product that is ideal for constructing note boards of all sizes. Once the board is cut, cover it with plain linen fabric, then accessorize it with stitched paper letters, flowers and other personalized embellishments.

MATERIALS AND TOOLS

CARDSTOCK: YELLOW, IVORY

LINEN FABRIC

DECORATIVE FABRICS
(IN THREE COORDINATING PATTERNS)

FELT (TO COVER BACK OF BOARD)

HOMOSOTE BOARD

SCISSORS

UTILITY KNIFE

FABRIC GLUE

DOUBLE-SIDED FUSIBLE WEB (STEAM-A-SEAM 2)

PLASTIC LETTER STENCIL TEMPLATES

FLOWER TEMPLATE

UPHOLSTERY NAILS

PENCIL

RULER

STAPLE GUN

IRON

SEWING MACHINE AND THREAD (OPTIONAL)

1 CUT HOMOSOTE BOARD

Using a utility knife, cut a piece of homosote board to the desired size for your note board. (Some stores may be able to cut the board for you.) After making the initial cut with the utility knife, continue to score the edges until you achieve a clean break.

2 MEASURE LINEN

Measure linen to cover the board, allowing 2½" (6cm) of extra fabric on all four sides. Pull the fabric taut over each edge of the board, then mitre the corners and staple in place with a staple gun.

▶3 BACK FABRIC WITH FUSIBLE WEB

Fuse a sheet of fusible web to the wrong side of a piece of decorative fabric (see Using Fusible Web, page 15).

▶4 CUT OUT FABRIC LETTERS

Using a letter template, trace the letters *N, O, T, E* and *S* in reverse onto the fusible-web side of the decorative fabric. Cut out each letter with scissors.

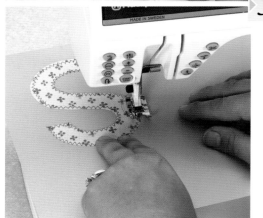

▶5 MOUNT LETTERS ONTO CARDSTOCK

Peel the carrier sheet off the fabric letters, and fuse the letters to sheets of yellow and ivory cardstock with an iron. For extra embellishment, use a sewing machine to zig-zag stitch around the the edges of each mounted letter.

▶6 ADD LETTERS TO BOARD

Cut the letters out, leaving a ¼" (6mm) border of cardstock around the fabric letter. When finished, tack the letters in place on the board with upholstery nails.

▶ 7 MAKE DECORATIVE FLOWERS

Fuse two pieces of fabric together with fusible web. Using a flower pattern, trace several flowers onto one side of the fused fabric. Cut the flowers out, then cut a fabric circle for the center of each flower.

▶ 8 ADD FLOWERS TO BOARD

Tack the flowers onto the board with upholstery nails, placing them as desired.

▶ 9 COVER BACK

Cut a piece of felt to cover the back of the board. Glue the felt in place, then trim any excess felt along the edges.

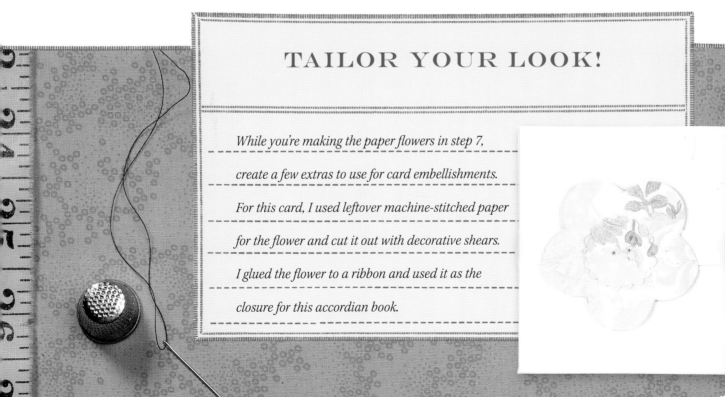

TAILOR YOUR LOOK!

While you're making the paper flowers in step 7, create a few extras to use for card embellishments. For this card, I used leftover machine-stitched paper for the flower and cut it out with decorative shears. I glued the flower to a ribbon and used it as the closure for this accordian book.

Crazy Frame

THIS FRAME TAKES ITS INSPIRATON from the "crazy quilt" aesthetic. Crazy quilts, which are made with scraps of miscellaneous fabric, feature irregular, non-uniform designs. For this project, break out your collection of leftover fabric paper scraps. Don't worry if your scraps are a mishmash of colors and patterns—the more variety you have, the more interesting your "crazy frame" will be! Each frame is unique, resembling something you might purchase in a charming, artsy boutique.

MATERIALS AND TOOLS

PHOTOGRAPH TO FRAME (PREFERABLY A
PHOTOCOPY, AS YOU WILL BE GLUING DIRECTLY
ON THE PHOTOGRAPH)

6" (15CM) MDF (MEDIUM DENSITY FIBERBOARD)
CIRCLE FRAME (AVAILABLE AT CRAFT STORES)

TWO SHEETS CARDSTOCK

SCRAPS OF COORDINATING FABRICS
AND FABRIC PAPERS

SCALLOP SHEARS

SCISSORS

PAPER GLUE

BASTING GLUE

PENCIL

SEWING MACHINE AND THREAD

1 CUT FABRIC PAPER

Cut scraps of fabric paper into random
square shapes using scallop shears.

2 GLUE FABRIC SQUARES ONTO CARDSTOCK

Place a dab of basting glue on the back of each
fabric square, then adhere the squares to a sheet
of cardstock in a random quilt-like pattern. It is
okay if the edges of the fabric squares overlap.

3 SEW FABRIC SQUARES TO CARDSTOCK

Using a sewing machine, secure the fabric paper squares to the cardstock by zig-zag stitching a series of diagonal rows across the sheet of cardstock. When finished, zig-zag stitch another series of diagonal rows in the opposite direction to create a diamond pattern across the surface, as shown.

4 TRACE FRAME ONTO PAPER

Trace the shape of the frame onto the machine-stitched fabric paper, tracing along both the inside and outside perimeter of the circle.

5 CUT OUT PAPER FRAME

Poke a hole in the center of the fabric paper with scissors. Use scallop shears to cut out the paper frame, trimming along the lines from step 4.

6 ADHERE PAPER FRAME TO FRAME BASE

Using paper glue, adhere the paper frame to the MDF frame base.

7 ASSEMBLE FRAME

Place the frame over the photograph to determine how you want to crop the image. Trim the photograph as necessary, then glue the frame on top of the photo as desired.

8 ADD BACKING

Cut a piece of cardstock to fit over the back of the frame, then glue the cardstock backing in place.

SEW EASY TIP

When cutting the inner portion of a frame with decorative scissors, experiment a bit to get the look you want. Here, by cutting counter-clockwise around the circle, the points of the scallops draw attention to the image in the frame. Cutting clockwise with the scalloped scissors will produce a softer effect.

Twin Canvas Frame

SOMETIMES, A LITTLE BIT OF "OUTSIDE-THE-BOX" THINKING goes a long way. That was the case for this project, where I experimented with some new uses for a store-bought, prestretched canvas. The result is a pair of clever shadow frames, hinged with pretty ribbons. You would never guess that each frame is actually the back of a canvas! This project, which requires minimal sewing, uses fun fabric, ribbon and ric-rac to gussy up some of your favorite mementos and other ephemera.

MATERIALS AND TOOLS

PHOTOGRAPH(S) AND EPHEMERA

TWO 9" x 12" (23CM X 30CM) PAINTING CANVASES, STRETCHED ON WOODEN FRAMES

COORDINATING DECORATIVE PAPER

COORDINATING FABRIC PIECES

FOAMCORE BOARD

CHIPBOARD

BUTTON THREAD

RIBBON

LACE

RIC-RAC

NEEDLE

SCISSORS

HOT KNIFE TOOL

FABRIC GLUE

PAPER GLUE

INDUSTRIAL-STRENGTH GLUE

ACRYLIC PAINT: IVORY, PINK

BROWN ANTIQUING GEL

INK (TEA DYE)

¾" (19MM) WASH BRUSH

1" (3 CM) STENCIL BRUSH

SPONGE OR SPONGE STICK

VINTAGE BUTTONS

PHOTO CORNERS

UPHOLSTERY TACKS

SOFT PAPER TOWELS

RULER

SMALL HAMMER

SCREW EYES

1 BASECOAT CANVASES

Using a ¾" (19mm) wash brush, coat both canvases with ivory acrylic paint. Allow the paint to dry completely.

2 PAINT CANVASES

Load a stencil brush with pink acrylic paint. Apply the paint to the canvas in a blotting motion.

▶ *3* STAIN CANVASES

Dilute antiquing gel with water, making a mixture of one part water to four parts gel. Dip a paper towel into the stain mixture, then gently apply the stain to the front and back of the canvases. Wipe off excess stain with another paper towel. Keep in mind that the more stain you apply, the darker the canvas will be. Let the stain dry completely.

▶ *4* CUT AND COVER FOAMCORE

Cut two sheets of foamcore with a hot knife tool, one to fit inside each wooden frame opening. Cut two pieces of fabric, making each piece 2" (5cm) larger than the foamcore sheets. Place the fabric on your work surface, face down, then center one foamcore piece on top of one fabric piece. Adhere the fabric to the foamcore using fabric glue, pulling the fabric taut over the edges and securing with glue. Cover the other piece of foamcore in the same manner.

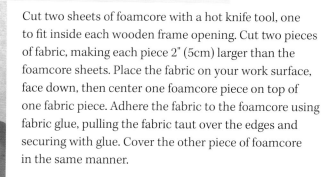

▶ *5* INSERT FOAMCORE INTO FRAME

Glue the fabric-covered foamcore into the frame openings using fabric glue.

▶ *6* TEAR AND AGE DECORATIVE PAPERS

Tear a sheet of decorative paper into a desired shape. Load a sponge or sponge stick with dye ink, then rub the loaded sponge along the edges of the paper to achieve an aged appearance.

7 COMPLETE PANELS

Adhere the collage components to the panels as desired. For the left panel, I adhered the aged decorative paper, a photo with photo corners and a Memories tag to the surface with paper glue. For the right panel, I adhered a photograph (mounted on chipboard) with photo corners, lace and a ric-rac embellishment (see Sew Easy Tip, below).

8 EMBELLISH CORNERS

Embellish the corners with buttons and/or upholstery tacks. Buttons can be adhered with industrial-strength glue, and upholstery tacks can be pounded in place with a hammer.

9 ATTACH FRAMES

Insert three screw eyes into the side of each frame. On the frame that is to be the left panel, place the screw eyes along the right edge; on the right panel, place the screw eyes along the left edge, so that both sets of screw eyes match up. Once the screw eyes are in place, join the two frames together by running a ribbon through each set of screw eyes and tying securely.

SEW EASY TIP

Ric-rac embellishments are a fun addition to any project—and they are easy to make! Cut a 13" (33cm) length of ric-rac. Thread a needle with an 18" (46cm) length of button thread and make a running stitch through the middle of the ric-rac between the points. Pull both ends of the thread together tightly. You will end up with a ric-rac embellishment that looks like a button. Secure the button thread by running it through the ric-rac several times and then knotting it off. Glue a bead or very small button to the middle of the embellishment for added variety.

ARE YOU A PROUD PARENT? A DOTING GRANDPARENT? An enthusiastic aunt or uncle? If so, consider creating this baby shadow box for the newest addition to the family. Baby-themed projects are always fun to make. This sweet and simple project is perfect for the arrival of a new baby or a wee one's first birthday. For the design, choose vintage prints, soft colors and childhood-themed embellishments. And, for an extra sentimental touch, include old family photographs of moms and babes.

MATERIALS AND TOOLS

PHOTOGRAPHS AND IMAGES (FROM VINTAGE WORKSHOP "LITTLE ONES" CD-ROM AND MORE EPHEMERA CD-ROM)

14" (36CM) SQUARE OPEN SHADOW BOX FRAME

SEVERAL SHEETS CARDSTOCK (CREAM AND 5-7 COORDINATING PATTERNS)

COORDINATING DECORATIVE PAPER

COORDINATING FABRIC

EMBROIDERY FLOSS: GREEN

EMBROIDERY NEEDLE

T-PIN

SCISSORS

PINKING SHEARS

SCALLOP SHEARS

ROTARY CUTTER WITH A STRAIGHT BLADE

FABRIC GLUE

PAPER GLUE

ACRYLIC PAINT: LIGHT IVORY

1" (3CM) WASH BRUSH

¾" (19MM) MOTHER-OF-PEARL BUTTONS

HEART TEMPLATE

SANDPAPER

CLOTH (TO WIPE OFF FRAME)

RULER

STAPLER

PENCIL

SEWING MACHINE AND THREAD

PHOTOCOPIER

1 SAND AND PAINT FRAME

Sand the surface of the frame and wipe clean. Paint the entire frame with light ivory acrylic paint. Allow the paint to dry completely, then add another coat.

2 COVER CARDSTOCK WITH STITCHED STRIPS

Use a rotary cutter with a straight blade to cut five to seven 1½" (4cm) strips of coordinating decorative cardstock. Line up the strips, edge to edge, on a sheet of cardstock, then staple each strip in place. Machine stitch the strips to the cardstock, using a zig-zag stitch along each common edge where two strips meet.

3 TRACE HEART

Using a heart frame template, trace the interior and exterior perimeter of the heart onto the stitched paper.

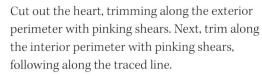

4 CUT OUT THE HEART FRAME

Cut out the heart, trimming along the exterior perimeter with pinking shears. Next, trim along the interior perimeter with pinking shears, following along the traced line.

NOTE: *To begin cutting the interior opening, you can cut a line right from the outer edge to the interior; once the heart is glued down, you will not see the cut.*

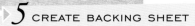

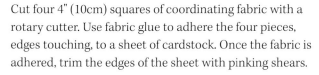

5 CREATE BACKING SHEET

Cut four 4" (10cm) squares of coordinating fabric with a rotary cutter. Use fabric glue to adhere the four pieces, edges touching, to a sheet of cardstock. Once the fabric is adhered, trim the edges of the sheet with pinking shears.

NOTE: *Instead of gluing the fabric to the cardstock, you can stitch it to the cardstock; this will add a decorative look.*

6 FRAME PHOTOGRAPH

Use paper glue to adhere the heart frame to the photograph, cropping as desired. Trim the excess paper around the frame. Center the framed photograph on the backing sheet made in step 5, then glue it in place.

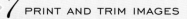

7 PRINT AND TRIM IMAGES

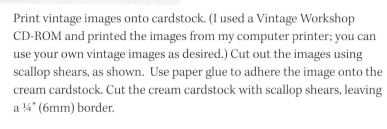

Print vintage images onto cardstock. (I used a Vintage Workshop CD-ROM and printed the images from my computer printer; you can use your own vintage images as desired.) Cut out the images using scallop shears, as shown. Use paper glue to adhere the image onto the cream cardstock. Cut the cream cardstock with scallop shears, leaving a ¼" (6mm) border.

8 EMBROIDER BORDERS

Use a T-pin to poke evenly spaced holes around the perimeter of the image. Run embroidery floss through the holes to embroider the border of the image, using a backstitch (see Making a Backstitch, page 14).

9 LINE INTERIOR SURFACE OF SHADOW BOX

Cut a sheet of decorative paper to the size of the shadow box interior. Use paper glue to adhere the paper to the interior surface.

10 MAKE STITCHED STRIP

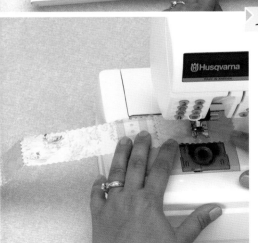

Using pinking shears or a rotary cutter with a pinking blade, cut sheets of different decorative paper into ten 1½" (4cm) squares. Machine stitch the paper squares together using a zig-zag stitch; you will now have a "paper ribbon" of stitched strips.

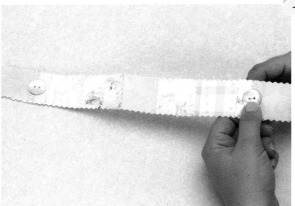

▶ *11* SEW BUTTONS TO STRIP

Fold under each end of the strip so it fits into the shadow box (widthwise). Sew one button to each end of the strip.

▶ *12* ADHERE STRIP TO BOX

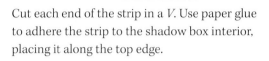

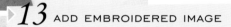

Cut each end of the strip in a *V*. Use paper glue to adhere the strip to the shadow box interior, placing it along the top edge.

▶ *13* ADD EMBROIDERED IMAGE

Adhere the embroidered image (from steps 7 and 8) to the shadow box interior, gluing it directly over the center of the strip.

▶ *14* ADD PHOTOGRAPH

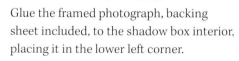

Glue the framed photograph, backing sheet included, to the shadow box interior, placing it in the lower left corner.

15 MAKE PAPER BOW

Cut two 1" (3cm) strips of decorative paper using a rotary cutter with a scallop blade. Bring both ends of one paper strip under to make two loops. Place the second strip around the center to secure the loops and glue in place.

16 ATTACH PAPER BOW

Cut an 8½" (22cm) strip for the tail. Glue the tail to the back of the bow. Adhere the paper bow to the shadow box interior.

17 ADD FINAL EMBELLISHMENT

Adhere the final embellishments, placing as desired.

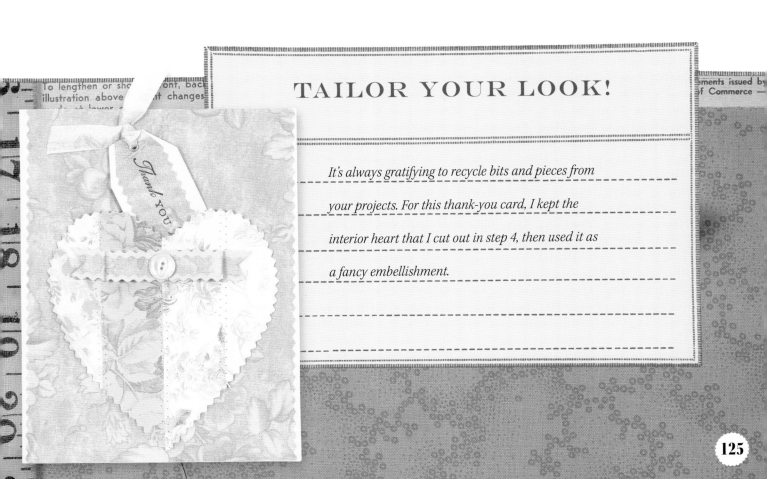

TAILOR YOUR LOOK!

It's always gratifying to recycle bits and pieces from your projects. For this thank-you card, I kept the interior heart that I cut out in step 4, then used it as a fancy embellishment.

RESOURCES

Whenever possible, please support your local craft shops by purchasing your tools and supplies from them. Their knowledgeable staff can assist you and answer most any question. Because not every store will have everything you need, I have provided the manufacturer's information for the products that were used in this book.

{3 RING CIRCLES}
423-639-0911
www.3ringcircles.com
MDF circle

{ANNA GRIFFIN, INC.}
888-817-8170
www.annagriffin.com
papers

{BEACON ADHESIVES}
914-699-3405
www.beaconadhesives.com
general craft glues

{DAISY D'S PAPER}
888-601-8955
www.daisydspaper.com
paper

{DELTA/RUBBER STAMPEDE}
www.deltacrafts.com
*acrylic paints, rubber stamps,
antiquing varnish*

{DESIGN ORIGINALS}
800-877-7820
www.d-originals.com
*More Ephemera CD-ROM
(ephemera and old photos)*

{DMC}
www.dmc-usa.com
embroidery floss, stencils

{FIBER SCRAPS}
215-230-4905
www.fiberscraps.com
tinted walnut ink

{FISKARS BRANDS, INC.}
866-348-5661
www.fiskars.com
*scissors, cutters, trimmers,
self-healing mats, hand drills*

{K&COMPANY}
888-244-2083
www.kandcompany.com
papers, stickers, frames

**{HUSQVARNA VIKING/
VSM SEWING INC.}**
800-358-0001
www.husqvarnaviking.com
** A Husqvarna Viking sewing machine was
used to create the projects in this book.*

**{JACQUARD PRODUCTS/
RUPERT, GIBBON & SPIDER}**
800-442-0455
www.jacquardproducts.com
*Pearl-Ex pigment powders,
Lumiere inks, acrylic ink*

{KRYLON PRODUCTS}
216-566-2200
www.krylon.com
spray varnish, leaf pens

{LOEW-CORNELL}
www.loew-cornell.com
paintbrushes

{ME AND MY BIG IDEAS}
949-583-2065
www.meandmybigideas.com
embellishments, papers

**{MELISSA FRANCES/
HEART & HOME}**
905-686-9031
www.melissafrances.com
*miniature cookie cutters,
resin embellishments*

{MICHAEL MILLER FABRICS}
212-704-0774
www.michaelmillerfabrics.com
fabric paper

**{MODA FABRICS/
UNITED NOTIONS}**
800-527-9447
www.unitednotions.com
cotton fabrics

{RIT DYE/PHOENIX BRANDS}
866-794-0800
www.ritdye.com
fabric dyes

{TARA MATERIALS}
www.taramaterials.com
stretched canvas

{TSUKINEKO, INC.}
425-883-7733
www.tsukineko.com
ink pads and cleaner

{THE VINTAGE WORKSHOP}
913-341-5559
www.thevintageworkshop.com
*copyright-free images,
antique images on CD-ROM*

{WALNUT HOLLOW FARMS, INC.}
800-950-5101
www.walnuthollow.com
*wooden products (frames, keepsake
boxes, memory albums, letters),
Makins Clay, creative textile tools, tags*

{THE WARM COMPANY}
206-320-9276
www.warmcompany.com
*Steam-A-Seam 2 Fusible Web,
needled cotton batting*

INDEX

THE BEST IN CREATIVE INSTRUCTION AND INSPIRATION IS FROM NORTH LIGHT BOOKS!

Author Heidi Boyd shows you how to create 50 step-by-step projects, including everything from purses, cards and holiday ornaments to barrettes and baby clothes. Even complete beginners will find success creating projects in the romantic style popular in magazines such as *Martha Stewart Living*. A wealth of no-sew projects—along with patterns and templates—make it a snap for you to get started right away!

ISBN 1-58180-592-6 ISBN 13: 978-1-58140-592-5
paperback 128 pages 33107

In her latest book, MaryJo McGraw brings the hottest scrapbooking techniques to the world of handcrafted cards. She makes it fun and easy for papercrafters and scrapbookers to work with stunning 3D embellishments to craft creative, elegant cards. With 26 step-by-step projects and more than 40 variations to choose from, crafters of all skill levels will find inspiration. The book also includes a handy "Getting Started" section that covers all of the basic materials and techniques.

ISBN 1-58180-628-0 ISBN 13: 978-1-58180-628-1
paperback 128 pages 33201

Beads give a sense of glamour and fun to everything—jewelry, fabrics and home décor. Author Heidi Boyd will inspire you with over 50 affordable and fashionable projects, including necklaces and bracelets, picture frames, journals and more. Beginners will learn basic beading and jewelry-making techniques, all of which are quick and easy. This book is part of the Simply Beautiful series, which features a simple yet sophisticated approach to popular crafts.

ISBN 1-58180-563-2 ISBN 13: 978-1-58180-563-5
paperback 128 pages 33108

Retro Mania! shows you how to make swell papercrafts using hot images and graphics from your favorite decades. You'll find 50 projects featuring popular decade-inspired motifs, from the swellegant 40s and fabulous 50s to the psychedelic 60s and groovy 70s. You'll love the stylish handmade cards, scrapbook pages and gift ideas. And you might even learn something along the way— the book is packed with fun facts about each era and includes tips on customizing every project to your personal swingin' taste.

These books and other fine North Light titles are available at your local fine art retailer or bookstore or from online suppliers.

ISBN 1-58180-746-5 ISBN 13: 978-1-58180-746-2
paperback 96 pages 33418